Christians need to know that there are solid answers to questions all of us should be asking. This book will help us to be better grounded in the faith personally, but equally important, it will help us answer questions skeptics are prone to ask. Enjoy the journey of studying this book!

—**Dr. Erwin W. Lutzer, Senior Pastor**
The Moody Church, Chicago

●

The Bible records over 150 questions that escaped the lips of our Lord. Like Him, my friend Robert Jeffress is always probing, asking life's most important questions so that we all might be "ready to give account of the hope that is within us." The answer to *How Can I Know?* is a simple one . . . Get a copy, read it, and reap!

—**O. S. Hawkins, President/CEO**
GuideStone Financial Resources

●

With a deft touch and a keen sensitivity to the questions faced by a lay audience, pastor Robert Jeffress of the far-famed First Baptist Dallas provides answers to seven critically important questions often asked by Christians. The remarkable thing about this book is the transformation of intensely academic ideas into the parlance of the average reader. This book is a major contribution for the churches.

—**Paige Patterson, President**
Southwestern Baptist Theological Seminary

●

As never before, our culture needs adequate biblical answers for the burning questions of faith and doubt. Robert Jeffress has been uniquely gifted by God to speak to our world from the authority of God's Word. His commitment to truth is obvious and his communication is clear. I have no doubt God will use this book to bring many to Himself and to help others find their way back to Him.

—**Mark L. Bailey, President**
Dallas Theological Seminary

HOW CAN I KNOW?

ANSWERS TO LIFE'S 7 MOST IMPORTANT QUESTIONS

ROBERT JEFFRESS

WORTHY®
PUBLISHING

Worthy
Hachette Book Group
1290 Avenue of the Americas, New York, NY 10104
worthypublishing.com
twitter.com/worthypub

First Edition: January 2013

Worthy is a division of Hachette Book Group, Inc. The Worthy name and logo are trademarks of Hachette Book Group, Inc.

The publisher is not responsible for websites (or their content) that are not owned by the publisher.

Unless otherwise noted, Scripture quotations are taken from the NEW AMERICAN STANDARD BIBLE®, © The Lockman Foundation 1960, 1962, 1963, 1968, 1971, 1972, 1973, 1975, 1977, 1995. Used by permission. Other Scripture quotations are taken from the following sources: The Holy Bible, New International Version®, NIV®. Copyright © 1973, 1978, 1984, 2011 by Biblica, Inc.™ Used by permission of Zondervan. All rights reserved worldwide. www.zondervan.com. The New King James Version (NKJV). © 1982 by Thomas Nelson, Inc. Used by permission. All rights reserved. The King James Version of the Bible (KJV). Public domain. J. B. Phillips: THE NEW TESTAMENT IN MODERN ENGLISH, Revised Edition (PHILLIPS). © J. B. Phillips 1958, 1960, 1972. Used by permission of Macmillan Publishing Co., Inc. The Living Bible (TLB). © 1971. Used by permission of Tyndale House Publishers, Inc., Wheaton, Illinois 60189. All rights reserved.

Cover design by Christopher Tobias
Print book interior design by Kimberly Sagmiller, Fudge Creative

Library of Congress Control Number: 2012951797

ISBNs: 978-1-93603-459-8 (trade paperback), 978-1-61795-162-6 (e-book)

Printed in the United States of America
LSC-H
Printing 13, 2021

To the Jim Donald family—Jim, Geneva, and Jennifer—for your vision and generous help in spreading God's eternal truth through our *Pathway to Victory* radio and television ministry.

Contents

No book is ever the result of one person. I am deeply indebted to . . .

Byron Williamson and his team at Worthy Publishing for the privilege of working with you on another significant project.

Bill Craig and his team at Lifeway Christian Resources for immediately catching the vision for this project and creating the curriculum material for *How Can I Know?*

Jennifer Stair for your meticulous review of every line of this manuscript and your helpful suggestions.

Rhonda Lowry for your assistance in tracking down and verifying all of the information for the endnotes.

Cecil Price for assisting me with the supplemental research for this project.

Sealy Yates, my friend and literary agent for eighteen years, for your practical advice and encouragement.

John Grable and the media team at First Baptist Dallas for your creativity in recording and packaging this material for a worldwide audience.

Carrilyn Baker, my administrative assistant for twelve years, for helping me with myriad details related to this project. I will never forget the leap of faith you and Scott took in leaving your home in Wichita Falls, Texas, to come work alongside us in Dallas.

My wife, Amy, an incredibly gifted writer who could be penning her own books if she were not so committed to helping me in my ministry.

The members of First Baptist Dallas for never wavering in your prayerful support of your pastor.

CHAPTER ONE

HOW CAN I KNOW THERE IS A GOD?

I was saved by God when I was five years old. I was called by God into the ministry when I was fifteen. I made a pledge to God to remain faithful to my bride when I was twenty-one.

I serve God by pastoring a large church. I write and talk about God to a lot of people. I converse with God every morning, night, and throughout the day.

Occasionally, I wonder if God really exists.

And I imagine you do too.

I regularly encounter people in my church who won't admit to having any doubts about anything, including the existence of God. "I may have questioned a lot of things, but I have *never* doubted that there is a God who loves me," they proclaim. These people seem to represent the vast majority of Americans who profess belief in God. According to a recent Gallup poll, nine in ten Americans say they believe in God.[1] Apparently Americans are much more inclined to believe in God than the rest of the world's population. Just over half (51 percent) of people worldwide claim to believe in God's existence.[2] However, I'm not sure that people are as sure about God's existence as they profess.

Daniel Dennett, author of *Darwin's Dangerous Idea*, is representative of the new atheists who have launched a vitriolic attack against so-called theists. As much as I disagree with just about everything Dennett believes, I think he is correct in clarifying the distinction between actual belief in God and what he terms "belief in belief."[3] If you more deeply question those nine in ten Americans who say they believe in God, you will find that what they really believe in is not God but their own beliefs about God. If they truly believed in God, wouldn't they conduct their lives differently? And if over half of the world's population and 90 percent of Americans acted as if God really existed and would one day evaluate their lives, wouldn't this world be in much better shape than its current state? Even atheists like Dennett can get it right every now and then!

Whether we are willing to admit it or not, most all of us have wondered about the existence of God. The only people who never doubt are those who never really think. I agree with Mark Buchanan's assertion: "The depth of our doubt is roughly proportional to the depth of our faith. Those with strong faith have equally strong doubts. That principle bears out in the other direction as well: People with a trivial and shallow faith usually have trivial and shallow doubts."[4]

This book is for those of you who have sincere questions about religion but may be too embarrassed to voice them. Perhaps you have grown up attending church and realize you should know the right answers to these questions—but you don't. And even if you feel confident in your own beliefs, you would be hard-pressed to answer questions from a friend, coworker, or family member such as:

- "How do you know the Bible is really true?"
- "How do you know Christianity is the right religion?"
- "How do you know there is such a thing as life after death?"

Maybe you picked up this book because although you would like to be a better person—maybe even a religious person—you have some legitimate doubts that have kept you from embracing Christianity. If so, you can relax. Rather than berating you for your doubts, I will address them intelligently and compassionately.

Questioning foundational beliefs is not a sin but a necessary pre-requisite for faith.

Obviously, the most foundational question about faith is the one we begin with in this chapter: how can we know there is a God?

WHY WE DOUBT THE EXISTENCE OF GOD

Why do people—believers and nonbelievers—question the reality of God? I believe there are five major sources of doubts about God.

Natural Doubt

You can tell your child that the tooth fairy exists and describe her beauty, kindness, and concern for children who are dentally challenged. You can even leave apparent evidence of her existence under your child's pillow (after you've traumatized your child by tying the loose tooth to a knob and slamming the door shut—remember that?). But sooner or later your child catches on that the tooth fairy is imaginary. And from there it is just a short journey to natural doubt about the Big Man Upstairs (I'm referring, of course, to Santa Claus).

Let's face it: it's hard to believe in an invisible being no matter what other people claim about that being. If God would appear visibly so everyone could see Him, surely that would be enough to silence our doubts. I know, I know. God *did* appear to the Israelites in the form of a cloud and to others in the person of Jesus Christ two thousand years ago, and people didn't believe. But I wasn't around back then, and I'm confident that those supernatural manifestations would have been enough for me (at least, that's what I tell myself).

I believe that God not only understands but empathizes with the natural challenge of believing in and committing our lives to Someone we have never seen. My belief is not based on some warm imaginative thought about what I hope God is like but on what He has said about the subject of doubt. Tucked away in a small book of the New Testament that most people flip past as they race to Revelation are these words from God spoken through Jude: "Be merciful to those who doubt" (Jude 22 NIV). Those six words reveal God's empathy toward those of us who occasionally question the reality of a Being we've not yet seen but have committed our lives to serving.

Philosophical Doubt

Some people doubt the existence of God on philosophical grounds. The most often cited philosophical argument against God is the existence of evil and suffering in the world. Eighteenth-century Scottish philosopher David Hume attempted to discredit Christianity by his now-famous dilemma: "Is God willing to prevent evil, but not able? Then he is impotent. Is he able, but not willing? Then he is malevolent. Is he both able and willing? Whence then is evil?"[5]

Hume claims that there are only three explanations for evil in the world: First, God would like to prevent evil but can't because He is impotent. The second choice is that God is able to prevent evil but chooses not to, making Him evil. If God is neither impotent nor evil, then the only logical conclusion is that He doesn't exist, since evil is a reality in the world. Of course, there is another explanation that Hume conveniently omits—we will explore it in chapter 4.

Experiential Doubt

We tend to be prisoners of our own experience. If we grew up in a family that did not believe in God, we will be prone to question the existence of a divine being. Certainly there are some notable exceptions to that general rule. Some years ago I invited William Murray, the son of the late atheist Madalyn Murray O'Hair, to share with our congregation his story about his conversion to Christianity. Watching the unhappiness and inconsistencies in his mother drove Murray to reject her belief system—which in this case was her disbelief in God.

However, the experience that leads many people to deny the existence of God is being disappointed by God. The loss of a child, the betrayal by a mate, the abuse by a parent, or the reality of unanswered prayers lead some to the conclusion that there is no God. Ted Turner, the media mogul who founded CNN, traces his rejection of Christianity to watching his sister die after he pleaded with God to save her life.[6]

Spiritual Doubt

We tend to assume that most atheists are intellectual giants who have examined all of the philosophical and scientific evidence for God and, after much deliberation, have concluded that He cannot exist. We sometimes harbor a secret fear that perhaps the atheist has discovered some smoking gun that proves once for all that there is no God.

I admit that sometimes I fall victim to that fear. Not long ago I went on a national cable news show to debate the president of the American Atheists Association. For a brief moment prior to the interview I was apprehensive, wondering what fiery dart the atheist would pull from his intellectual arsenal to shoot down my arguments. I need not have worried. His tepid arguments only reinforced what I have always known to be true: atheists tend to reject God for spiritual rather than intellectual reasons.

The apostle Paul reminded the Roman Christians that evidence for God's existence is available to all people:

> For the wrath of God is revealed from heaven against all ungodliness and unrighteousness of men who suppress the truth in unrighteousness, because that which is known about God is evident within them; for God made it evident to them. For since the creation of the world His invisible attributes, His eternal power and divine nature, have been clearly seen, being understood through what has been made, so that they are without excuse. (Romans 1:18–20)

As we will see in the next section, the evidence for God in the cosmos is overwhelming. So why do people ignore that evidence? Paul continues,

> For even though they knew God, they did not honor Him as God or give thanks, but they became futile in their speculations, and their foolish heart was darkened. (Romans 1:21)

Although atheists have received a general knowledge of God through creation, they have intentionally rejected that knowledge. Why? If there is a divine Creator who made us, then it is only reasonable to conclude we must submit to Him—something an atheist is unwilling to do. Contrary to popular belief, atheists are not earnestly scouring the universe for any evidence of God so that they might believe. An atheist has no more interest in finding God than a thief has in finding a policeman. Instead, as Paul asserts, the atheist deliberately rejects the evidence for God that is all around him.

But he is not content just to reject the truth about God; the atheist must replace that truth with his own truth:

> Professing to be wise, they became fools, and exchanged the glory of the incorruptible God for an image in the form of corruptible man and of birds and four-footed animals and crawling creatures. (Romans 1:22–23)

Paul is referring to people who replace the worship of the true God with the worship of idols that reduce God to a manageable and nonthreatening deity. Atheists, and even many theists, engage in the same reductionism in order to eliminate the need for God, or at least to transform Him into a deity more to our liking.

When I read the phrase "an image in the form of . . . birds and four-footed animals and crawling creatures," I think immediately of the theory of evolution, which is an alternative faith-based explanation for the origin of life. Don't let anyone fool you: evolution has as much to say about the existence of God as creationism. The former is rooted in the presupposition that there is no God (or at least not one who had anything to do with the creation of life) and the latter starts with the assumption that "In the beginning God created . . ." Both evolutionists and creationists approach the question about the origin of life with specific assertions about God that require a great deal of faith.

Even many who claim to believe in God feel the need to refashion the God of the Bible. After Rabbi Harold Kushner lost his young son to disease, Kushner concluded that he could no longer believe in an omnipotent God who could intervene in human affairs but chose not to. Rabbi Kushner claimed that "even God has a hard time keeping chaos in check" and that "God is a God of justice and not of power."[7] Kushner's attempt to shrink God to a more intellectually manageable deity reminds me of the observation, "In the beginning God created man in His own image, and ever since that time man has been trying to repay the compliment!"

Empirical Doubt

Few atheists admit they are rejecting the abundant evidence for God for spiritual reasons. Instead, they try to convince people that science has driven the final nail into the coffin of theism. Richard Dawkins, another one of the "new atheists," claims in his best-selling book *The God Delusion* that it is impossible to be a scientific thinker and a theist. To substantiate his claim, he cites a 1998 study showing that only 7 percent of American scientists in the National Academy of Sciences believe in a personal God.[8]

The average person (who, according to the Gallup poll, most likely believes in God) is threatened by that statistic. He reasons that since scientists are smarter than he is and most scientists don't believe in God, then his belief in God must be rooted in fable rather than fact.[9]

However, such a conclusion is ill-founded for two reasons. First, the study fails to identify the cause-effect relationship between scientists and their beliefs. It's the "which came first: the chicken or the egg?" dilemma. Let's concede the fact that the majority of scientists are atheists or agnostics. Which came first: their pursuit of science or their rejection of God? People assume that scientists' atheism is the result of their being scientists. But couldn't they have just as easily started with a rejection of God and then pursued the study of science as an alternative explanation of the origin of the universe?

The second problem with concluding that belief in God is unscientific because so few scientists are theists is that this conclusion is circular reasoning. Let me explain. The scientific method requires observing and testing a hypothesis in nature. Only that which can be observed and measured in nature can qualify as a scientific explanation for why things are the way they are. The scientific method is based on *naturalism*—the assumption that nature is all there is and that the universe is a closed system. There is no allowance for the possibility that some things can only be explained by that which is "above nature" (the meaning of the word *supernatural*).

Such a self-imposed limitation in the pursuit of truth is the reason evolutionists have been successful in ensuring that their view of the origin of life is the only view presented in public education. Evolution is labeled as "science" since it is based on the natural, and creationism is labeled as "religion" because it is based on the supernatural. Secularists argue that evolution belongs in the school classroom and creationism belongs in the Sunday school classroom.

But wait a minute! Suppose for the sake of argument that there really is an invisible, transcendent being who is responsible for everything in the universe. Would not that reality be a scientific explanation for the origin of the universe, as well as a religious one? Yet by definition naturalism cannot allow for such an explanation, even if it is true. The scientist who bases his reasoning on naturalism says, "God cannot be the Creator of the universe because my belief system does not allow for the existence of a God who could create the universe." That is circular reasoning.

It is a profound mistake to allow scientists to get away with equating science with reality and then limiting science to that which is observable in nature—because the result is the widely accepted conclusion that reality is only that which is observable in nature. Philosopher Alvin Plantinga demonstrates the absurdity of such a circular argument:

> [It] is like the drunk who insisted on looking for his lost car keys only under the streetlight on the grounds that the light was better there. In fact, it would go the drunk one better; it would insist that because the keys would be hard to find in the dark, they must be under the light.[10]

To limit one's search for the truth about the origin of life to that which is "under the light" severely limits the honest inquiry of all possibilities. But such a self-imposed limitation in no way eliminates the possibility that the answer exists outside of that which can be seen.

CAN WE PROVE THE EXISTENCE OF GOD?

We must, however, concede one point to the naturalists. It is true that we cannot prove the existence of a supernatural, invisible being. However, there is a difference between *proof* and *evidence*. For example, as I am sitting at my computer typing these words I hear someone next door typing on a computer keyboard as well. I conclude it is my assistant Carrilyn, even though I can't see her. Why? First, the office next door is hers. Second, sixty seconds ago she called me from her extension next door. Third, the only time anyone else sits at her desks and types is when she is on vacation, and she is not on vacation. Based on this evidence can I *prove* that Carrilyn is the one typing at the keyboard? No. There is a possibility that it *could* be the president of the United States seated at Carrilyn's workstation. However, the evidence argues strongly for the fact that it is Carrilyn and not the president.

Similarly, while we cannot prove God's existence, we can look at evidence that strongly argues for His existence. Unfortunately, when confronted with the strong evidence for the existence of God some people willingly choose to ignore it. Jimmy Williams, founder of Probe Ministries, tells the story of a man who went to a psychiatrist convinced that he was dead. The psychiatrist tried everything to assure the patient that he was not dead. The patient remained undeterred in his belief. Finally, the psychiatrist asked him, "Do dead men bleed?" The patient said dead men do not bleed. The psychiatrist then pulled out a pocketknife, reached over, and nicked the man's finger. The patient exclaimed, "What do you know? Dead men *do* bleed!"[11]

While it is true that theists cannot prove the existence of God, it is equally true that atheists cannot prove God does *not* exist. Legal scholar and philosopher Mortimer Adler observed that while it is possible to prove an affirmative existential proposition, it is impossible to prove a negative existential proposition—that something does not exist. For example, someone might claim that a red eagle exists and someone else may assert that red eagles do not exist. The first person only needs to find one red eagle to prove his claim. However, the second person must scour every corner of this vast universe—an impossible feat—to ensure he has not missed a red eagle somewhere.[12]

When it comes to the existence of God, we must understand that the issue is not about proving whether God exists but about making an informed decision based on the evidence. In this chapter we are going to examine the four most powerful pieces of evidence for the existence of God. After weighing the evidence, an honest seeker of truth should ask himself, "Is it more reasonable to accept or deny that there is a God?"

THE COSMOLOGICAL ARGUMENT:
WHY IS THERE SOMETHING RATHER THAN NOTHING?

Look around you, carefully noting everything you see. A chair, a lamp, a tree outside the window, a cloud in the sky. Now ask yourself, "Why do I see *something* rather than nothing at all?" Or, to get even more introspective, "Why do I see?" And for a real mind-blowing question, "Why am I even asking myself this question?"

The naturalist's explanation for the existence of everything we see is found in this simple formula:

$$\text{No One} \times \text{Nothing} = \text{Everything}$$

Yet the existence of a vast universe (not to mention of you and me) strongly suggests that Someone brought something into existence out of nothing.

To put this argument into perspective, consider the immensity of our universe. Our solar system exists in the Milky Way Galaxy, which consists of at least 100 billion stars. The average distance between those stars is 30 trillion miles. How far is 30 trillion miles? Author Norman Geisler asks readers to imagine boarding one of the now-decommissioned space shuttles for a travel through the Milky Way Galaxy. The space shuttles flew at 17,000 miles per hour or five miles per second. At that speed, it would take you 201,450 years to travel 30 trillion miles.

Or put another way, if you had started your journey on the day of Christ's birth more than two thousand years ago, by now you would have just traveled one-hundredth of the way there. And once you finally arrived, you would have just made it to the first star, with hundreds of billions yet to go. And remember, that is just the Milky Way Galaxy. Our galaxy is just one of hundreds of billions of galaxies in the universe![13]

So how did these hundreds of billions of stars in hundreds of billions of galaxies come into existence? For many years atheists argued that the universe was eternal and, therefore, had always existed. The famous astronomer Carl Sagan begins his best-selling book *Cosmos* with these words: "The Cosmos is all that is or ever was or ever will be."[14] But obviously, galaxies, stars, and planets all had a beginning. If you were to trace everything in the universe back to its absolute beginning, there had to be some burst of energy that set everything into motion.

Interestingly, scientists now concede that the universe did have a beginning. After all, the second law of thermodynamics tells us that the universe is running out of usable energy. But if the universe is eternal, that means it has an infinite past. And if the universe has an infinite past, it would have already run out of energy by now. In the 1930s a Belgian priest-turned-astronomer named Georges Lemaître theorized that the entire universe was packed into a dense mass of matter that existed at temperatures of trillions of degrees. Then, about 13.7 billion years ago, this mass of matter exploded, creating the entire universe, which is continuing to expand. Lemaître himself described his theory as "the Cosmic Egg exploding at the moment of creation."[15] Later, astronomer and mathematician Sir Frederick Hoyle coined the term "the big bang," which continues today to be the most popular explanation for the origin of the universe.[16]

Respected astronomers like Edwin Hubble (for whom the famed Hubble telescope was named) confirmed that there are myriad other galaxies beyond our Milky Way Galaxy and that the universe is indeed expanding; therefore, the universe had a beginning like Lemaître theorized. Interestingly, on April 23, 1992, a team of scientists released findings from the Cosmic Background Explorer satellite (COBE) that confirmed what Hubble and Lemaître had theorized about the beginning of the universe: there was an explosion of matter that set the universe into motion.[17] Obviously, such a theory raises a number of serious questions for the naturalist.

First, from where did that dense mass of matter come? Scientists used to say that the dense mass of matter always existed. But is it logical to believe that something came out of nothing? To say that the universe is self-created is absurd because such a claim means that the universe (in the form of a dense mass of matter) had both to exist and not exist at the same time.

A closely related question is, what caused this expansion to occur? James Emory White uses the analogy of a row of dominoes. You've probably seen elaborate displays of falling dominoes in the form of a map or some other design that take many minutes to completely topple over. Imagine as you are flipping through the television channels, you stop as you watch such a news story showing collapsing dominoes. Although you missed the first part of the segment, you know that something or someone pushed that first domino to get the process started.

Such an obvious conclusion is what makes the big bang theory such a conundrum for atheists. Someone or something had to push the first domino and get the creation process started. To assert that the entire universe came from nothing and because of nothing is nonsensical. As skeptic David Hume wrote, "I never asserted so absurd a Proposition as that anything might arise without a cause."[18] It is a simple yet profound truth. Out of nothing comes . . . nothing.

Of course, those of us who believe that God created the universe believe that He did so *ex nihilo* (literally, "out of nothing"). He did not create the universe out of material that already existed (*ex materia*) or out of Himself (*ex Deo*). God is the eternal cause of everything that exists.

But isn't it contradictory to claim it is impossible for the universe (or the matter that exploded into the universe) to be eternal and without cause, and at the same time assert God is eternal and without cause?

Not at all. Both atheists and theists believe that whatever is eternal by definition does not need a cause. It has always existed and therefore has no cause. Only that which has a beginning needs an identifiable cause. For years the atheist believed that the "eternal something" was the universe (or the matter that exploded into the universe). The theist believes that the eternal something is God.

Unfortunately for the atheist, science has now demonstrated that the universe had a beginning, necessitating a cause. Furthermore, since the universe consists of time, space, matter, and energy, this cause must transcend time, space, matter, and energy. The cause must be above or beyond the natural—in other words, supernatural. (I realize I am using the terms *atheist* and *evolutionist* interchangeably. To be fair, not all evolutionists are atheists. However, I do not know of an atheist who is not an evolutionist. By definition, atheists can only embrace a natural, rather than supernatural, explanation for the origin of life and the universe.)

William Lane Craig argues that this eternal, transcendent cause must also be personal because how else could a timeless cause give rise to a temporal effect such as the universe? Craig uses the illustration of water freezing (the effect) when the temperature is below 0°C. If water were below 0°C from eternity past, it would be impossible for water to begin to freeze a finite time ago. If the cause is eternally present, so is the effect. "The only way for the cause to be timeless and the effect to begin in time is for the cause to be a personal agent who freely chooses to create an effect in time without any prior determining cause. . . . Thus we are brought not merely to a transcendent cause of the universe but to its personal Creator."[19]

Amazingly, even strident atheist Richard Dawkins admits that there might be some transcendent cause to explain the origin of the cosmos. "There could be something incredibly grand and incomprehensible and beyond our present understanding," Dawkins conceded in an interview with *Time* magazine. Asked if that "something incredibly grand" could be God, Dawkins replied, "Yes. But it could be any of a billion Gods. It could be the God of the Martians or the inhabitants of Alpha Centauri. The chance of it being a particular God, Yahweh the God of Jesus, is vanishingly small."[20] Author Mark Mittelberg offers a great rejoinder to Dawkins's response: "You can call Him what you want, but the evidence from the origin of the universe tells us a lot about what He is like—and the description sounds amazingly similar to what the Bible tells us about one particular God, who actually is called Yahweh, the God of Jesus, the Creator of the world."[21]

The often-asked question "If there is a God, why doesn't He reveal Himself so that everyone can believe in Him?" is built upon a false premise. God *has* revealed Himself in the world. The existence of anything and everything in the cosmos offers powerful evidence for the existence of God. As the psalmist declared, "The heavens declare the glory of God; the skies proclaim the work of his hands" (Psalm 19:1 NIV). When famed astronaut John Glenn was allowed to fly in the space shuttle *Discovery* at age seventy-seven, he looked out the window and remarked, "To look out at this kind of creation and not believe in God is to me impossible."[22]

While the existence of the universe is a powerful argument for a transcendent and personal Creator, atheist Richard Dawkins is correct in claiming that it is a giant leap from a First Cause to the God of the Bible. However, the Creator has left other fingerprints in the universe that tell us even more about Himself.

THE TELEOLOGICAL ARGUMENT:
HOW DO YOU EXPLAIN THE UNIVERSE'S COMPLEX DESIGN?

Author Dennis McCallum asks readers to suppose that there are two men riding on a railway coach who glance out of the window during one of the stops. They see numerous white stones on a hillside spelling out the words: THE CANADIAN RAILWAYS WELCOMES YOU TO CANADA. One of the men says, "Someone sure spent a lot of time and effort to arrange all those stones into that message." The second man disagrees. He claims there is no proof that anyone did anything to form that message with the rocks; they just fell into place by accident. After all, he notes, there are stones on other parts of the hill that form no message, and furthermore, the message is at the bottom of a slope, providing an explanation for how they rolled into place. No one can prove that these stones did not fall into this pattern by accident.

A few minutes later the second man says, "We had better go into the train station while we are stopped and exchange our US currency for Canadian money." "Why should we do that?" the first man asks. The second man points to the message on the hill and says, "Can't you read? It says we are entering Canada!"[23]

When confronted with the evidence for a Creator that comes from the complex design of the universe, atheists will argue that such design occurred by chance. Yet at the same time they are arguing the randomness of the universe, they also base their alternative theory for the origin of the universe on scientific laws that are based on order, not on chaos.

You can't have your philosophical cake and eat it too! Either the intricate design found in the universe is the result of random events that may or may not be repeatable, or it is the product of a Creator who has designed the universe to run according to observable and repeatable laws. The evidence that the design and order of the universe provide for the existence of God is often called the teleological argument for God (*teleos* means "design"). Where exactly do we see this design that argues for a Creator?

The Universe

The slightest variation in any number of constants would have made the initial expansion of the universe called the "big bang theory" impossible. Either the universe would have not expanded at all, or it would have expanded so rapidly that it would have become nothingness instantaneously.[24] The "big bang theory" postulates that by "chance" all of the conditions were just right for the universe to have come into existence.

The Earth

The design found in the universe is not limited to its beginning. The universe has been intricately designed to allow for life on our planet, even though the universe as a whole seems hostile to life. William Dembski writes, "Imagine you discover an abandoned cabin in the mountains. As you approach the cabin, you notice something strange. Your favorite meal is cooking in the oven, the TV is turned on to your favorite program, and all your favorite books, DVDs, and video games are lying on the table. What would you conclude? The best explanation would clearly be that someone was expecting your arrival. Scientists have recently learned that the universe is much like this cabin—it's crafted uniquely for us."[25] Scientists estimate there are more than one hundred conditions on our planet that form an astronomical/biological "welcome mat" for human beings, making the earth uniquely suited for human life.

The Size of Earth

Our planet's size is perfect for the existence of life. Were the earth smaller or larger, it would not have an atmosphere that could support the proper mixture of oxygen and nitrogen. The earth is located exactly the right distance from the sun to support human life. Were the earth any farther away from the sun, we would freeze to death. Were the earth closer to the sun, we would all burn up.

Water

Our bodies are two-thirds water. Water's unique properties make our existence possible. For example, water has an especially high boiling and low freezing point, allowing us to live with highly fluctuating temperatures. Water is chemically neutral, allowing for food, minerals, and medicines to be absorbed into our bodies.

Water is essential for all life, and our planet has an abundance of it. Ninety-seven percent of our planet's water supply is in the oceans. But the process of evaporation removes water from the oceans, leaves the salt behind, and disperses the water over the earth for the benefit of living beings and vegetation.[26]

Gravity

Physicists tell us that for life to exist on earth, the force of gravity must remain constant. In fact, if our planet's gravitational force were altered by one part in ten thousand billion billion billion relative to other forces, life could not exist on earth.[27] Furthermore, consider the gravitational relationship the earth has with the moon. If that force were any stronger, ocean tides would flood our planet.

Oxygen and Carbon Dioxide

Our atmosphere is comprised of 21 percent oxygen. If the percentage were higher, fires would ignite spontaneously across the planet. If the percentage were lower, we would suffocate. Similarly, if the carbon dioxide level were higher, the greenhouse effect would incinerate our planet. If the carbon dioxide level were lower, it would disrupt the essential process of photosynthesis for plants, making life on earth impossible.

How likely is is that these and the other constants necessary for life on earth would exist by chance? Astrophysicist Hugh Ross estimates there are 122 constants necessary to sustain life on our planet. Ross also estimates the number of planets in the universe to be 10^{22}

(that is 1 with 22 zeroes behind it). Therefore, Ross calculates that the chance of one planet in the universe containing all of these necessary constants to sustain life would be 10^{138} (or 1 followed by 138 zeroes). To help put this in perspective, scientists estimate there are "only" 10^{70} atoms in the entire universe. Thus, a one in 10^{138} probability of earth randomly containing all the constants necessary to sustain life represents a zero chance.[28]

The Cell

How did life begin? Charles Darwin believed that the first unicellular organism emerged from some primordial biotic soup by chance. Yet Darwin conceded that "if it could be demonstrated that any complex organ existed which could not possibly have been formed by numerous, successive, slight modifications, my theory would absolutely break down." As Michael Behe demonstrates in his book *Darwin's Black Box*, the cell is that complex organ that renders Darwin's theory untenable. Darwin, like other biologists of his day, failed to understand the complexity of the cell. Behe explains that a cell requires a number of functioning systems that must be present at once rather than evolving over a period of time, including a functioning membrane, a system to build the DNA units, a system to control the copying of DNA, and system for processing energy.[29]

What is the possibility of a fully functioning cell assembling itself together by chance? Cambridge University astronomer and mathematician Sir Frederick Hoyle writes, "The likelihood of the formation of life from inanimate matter is one to a number with 40,000 [zeroes] after it. . . . It is big enough to bury Darwin and the whole theory of evolution. . . . If the beginnings of life were not random, they must therefore have been the product of purposeful intelligence."[30]

The Human Body

Of course, human bodies consist of more than a single cell. The human body is comprised of thousands of complex organs and systems necessary to experience life as we know it. For example, consider your eyes. Each of your eyes is a ball with a lens on one side and, on the other side, a light-sensitive retina that consists of rods and cones. The lens is protected by a covering called the cornea and rests on an iris that is designed to protect the cornea from excessive light. Every four hours, a watery substance within the eye is replaced, while tear glands continually flush the outside of the eye clean. The eye also has its own "windshield wiper" called the eyelid that spreads a special secretion over the cornea to keep it moist and to protect it from dust.[31]

If that were not complicated enough, the eye does not exist by itself. As light hits the eye, billions of bits of information travel from the eye through millions of nerve fibers linked to the brain. There, at "information central" in the visual cortex of the brain, that data is processed and dispatched, along with various instructions.[32]

How do you explain the design and order in the universe, the earth, the cell, and the human body? Most atheists concede that there is observable design in nature, but they refuse to acknowledge that a design requires a designer. Instead, they attribute the design in nature to chance. Yet we have seen that the mathematical probability of either an inhabitable earth or a complex cell randomly occurring is effectively zero. What are the chances of *both* occurring randomly?

The atheist's answer to that seemingly insurmountable mathematical hurdle is what is called the multiple universe theory, which imagines that our universe is one of an infinite number of universes. In an infinite number of universes, any and every set of conditions will occur, including those we have discussed. To understand what the atheist is saying, consider this illustration. If you took all the hundreds of thousands of components of a 777 jumbo jetliner and placed them in a giant wind tunnel, the chances that they would assemble into a jet plane would be almost nonexistent. But what if you performed the experiment in an infinite number of wind tunnels? Eventually, so the theory goes, you could produce a fully assembled, functional 777 jet.

Here's the problem with such a theory. There is absolutely no evidence that there are an infinite number of universes. Furthermore, such a fanciful theory—taken to its natural conclusion—means that there is really no explanation for anything that happens in the world. Why does water freeze at 32^0 F, the earth revolve the sun, and summer follow spring? And even if they occur once, why do these phenomena keep occurring?

According to the multiple universe theory, the only explanation is that out of the infinite number of universes, we happen to be in the one where these things happen! As Norman Geisler writes, "The Multiple Universe Theory is simply a desperate attempt to avoid the implications of design. It doesn't multiply chances, it multiplies absurdities."[33]

William Paley used the parable of a man walking through a field and discovering a stone. He walks a little farther and discovers an ornate watch. The man reasonably concludes that the stone is simply the result of a sliver of mineral being chipped away by the process of erosion over a long period of time. But the beauty, symmetry, design, and purpose represented in the watch could not have happened by chance. The watch must be the product of an intelligent and purposeful Creator.[34]

Attempts to write off the complexity of our universe by such preposterous explanations as the multiple universe theory demonstrate how unwilling the atheist is to objectively consider the evidence for the existence of God. As the psalmist said, "The fool has said in his heart, 'There is no God'" (Psalm 14:1). To ascribe the complex design of the universe and all it contains to random chance is the essence of true foolishness.

THE ANTHROPOLOGICAL ARGUMENT: HOW DO YOU EXPLAIN YOU?

The anthropological argument for God is based on the presence of human beings (*anthropos* means "human") on the earth. Consider several unique aspects of human beings.

Your Existence

The atheist argues that all life forms, including human beings, are the result of slow changes or mutations that occurred over billions of years, beginning with a single-celled organism. But how did that single-celled organism come into existence? The atheist's explanation is that when chemicals such as ammonia, methane, and hydrogen covered the earth they were energized by lightning, resulting in the production of amino acids. Those amino acids randomly assembled to produce protein molecules that eventually resulted in the first one-celled creature.

Let's accept for a moment the atheist's hypothesis that amino acids are the result of lightning striking chemicals covering the earth billions of years ago. What are the chances of the right amino acids randomly assembling together to produce a single-protein molecule? Biochemists tell us that the probability of a single-protein molecule assembling together by chance is 1 in 10^{161} (that is a 1 followed by 161 zeroes). Remember, there are "only" 10^{70} atoms in the entire universe.

But to create a single cell you need more than the creation of a protein molecule. A living cell requires hundreds of protein molecules coming together to support life. Given the complexity of the cell—which could not have evolved over a period of time but had to have all its functioning parts operational from the beginning—the probability of a cell assembling together by chance is remote. As we saw in the last section, Sir Frederick Hoyle estimates that the chances of a single cell assembling itself randomly is 1 followed by 40,000 zeroes.

But even if a cell were able to come into existence randomly, you still just have unicellular creature. How does the evolutionist explain a single-celled creature evolving into a fully functioning human being with such intricately designed mechanisms as the eye or brain? His only answer is that given enough time simple life forms will evolve through slight changes into complex life forms. That is like saying, "Given enough time the car sitting in my garage will evolve into a massive luxury ocean liner."

The counterargument from the evolutionist will likely be, "That's a nonsensical argument because a car is an inanimate object and a cell is a living organism." True, but why couldn't an inanimate car come to life and start reassembling itself into an ocean liner? After all, the evolutionist's argument is that living matter evolved from nonliving matter.

Your Consciousness

Even if the evolutionary theory answered the question of human existence, how do we explain what some have called "the humanness of humans"? For example, why are we aware of our existence? As cosmologist Allan Sandage asks, "How is it that inanimate matter can organize itself to contemplate itself?"[35] The evolutionist answers that consciousness is simply the result of evolutionary development. Given enough time, there will be slight mutations until an organism develops an awareness of its existence. Yet such a declaration really does not answer the question. As J. P. Moreland concludes, "It will not do to claim that consciousness simply emerged from matter when it reached a certain level of complexity, because 'emergence' is merely a label for, and not an explanation of, the phenomena to be explained."[36]

Beyond our awareness of our own existence, human beings have an awareness of the existence of the supernatural. Since the beginning of mankind, humans in all cultures have demonstrated an innate desire to worship a deity. Some evolutionists have attempted to explain such desires as part of the evolutionary process.

However, the basis of evolution is natural selection (or "survival of the fittest"), which means that a desire for God could only be attributed to evolutionary development if such a desire promoted the survival of the species. While it is true that there are positive benefits that accrue to those who believe in God, it is equally true that many times those who believe in God act in a way that is contrary to their self-interest. Think about martyrs throughout history who sacrificed their lives because of their belief in God. They are contradictions of the foundational premise of evolution: the survival of the fittest.

Furthermore, the evolutionist's claim that mankind's belief in God is part of the genetic makeup that assists our survival presents another huge problem for the evolutionist. Since the atheist does not believe in God and yet ascribes our God-consciousness to evolutionary development, he is claiming that we are genetically programmed to believe a lie. But if we cannot trust what our minds lead us to believe about the existence of God, why should the evolutionist trust what his mind leads him to believe about science?

A better explanation for man's awareness of God is that such awareness is rooted in reality. C. S. Lewis famously argued that our desire for God is one of the most convincing arguments for the existence of God:

> Creatures are not born with desires unless satisfaction for those desires exists. A baby feels hunger; well, there is such a thing as food. A duckling wants to swim: well, there is such a thing as water. Men feel sexual desire: well, there is such a thing as sex. If I find in myself a desire which no experience in this world can satisfy, the most probable explanation is that I was made for another world.[37]

Your Morality

Beyond mankind's innate awareness of himself and of God, the consciousness of certain moral absolutes strongly argues for existence of God. The relationship between morality and the existence of God can be summarized this way:

1. Objective moral absolutes do not exist if God does not exist.
2. Objective moral values do exist.
3. Therefore, God exists.

If there is no Supreme Judge to declare what is right and wrong, then behavior we declare to be "wrong" is really a matter of personal preference. For example, most people would agree that raping a child is morally wrong. But on what basis do we make such a judgment? Some would answer, "Society has deemed that raping a child is wrong." But is society a reliable arbitrator of what is right and wrong? After all, certain societies in history have declared it permissible for human beings to own other human beings. Other cultures have judged it acceptable to exterminate entire races of people.

So if society cannot be trusted to provide objective moral standards to follow, from where do such standards originate? As Yale law professor Arthur Leff asked, "Who among us ought to be able to declare 'law' that ought to be obeyed? . . . Either God exists or He does not, but if He does not, nothing and no one can take His place."[38]

Of course, the evolutionist counters that our sense of morality is the result of our evolutionary development and is present in us only to aid our continued survival as a species. We have a desire to do good rather than evil because it is beneficial to our self-interest. Yet there is no scientific evidence to prove that our sense of right and wrong is the product of evolutionary development. But beyond the lack of any evidence, there are other problems with this alternative explanation for the existence of moral absolutes.

First, if our sense of right and wrong is simply the result of biological forces, then we have no basis for condemning the actions of other people. After all, if my choice not to rape a child is only attributable to a biological tendency I've inherited that promotes the well-being of my species, why should we condemn someone who does engage in that behavior? Isn't his action simply attributable to a variant in the genetic gene pool?

Second, how do you explain the altruistic actions of people if they are genetically predisposed to act in their own interests? For example, I have a friend who was driving home from church one rainy Sunday when he noticed cars stopped along the side of an overflowing creek. When he got out of the car, people told him that a young Chinese girl had been overtaken by the rushing water and was barely holding on to a tree limb. My friend risked his life to wade into the water and rescue the girl (her friend had already been swept away in the flood). How does evolution explain my friend's willingness to risk his life for another person? Wouldn't his inherited survival instinct tell him that he needed to keep on driving, rather than to intervene?

Furthermore, evolutionary theory says that humans have been programmed throughout history to be hostile to those outside their own people group. Yet my friend was willing to risk his life for the benefit of a girl who was a part of another people group. The existence of objective moral absolutes in humans, especially the inexplicable tendency toward altruism, argues strongly for a Creator God who instilled such a code of conduct in each of us.

THE EXPERIENTIAL ARGUMENT:
WHY DO PEOPLE FIND GOD IF HE DOESN'T EXIST?

Admittedly, the experiential argument offers the least amount of empirically verifiable evidence, yet it provides one of the most thought-provoking rationales for the existence of God. Consider the millions of people throughout history who claim to have experienced a personal relationship with God, despite great sacrifice or skepticism. For example, twelve apostles and more than five hundred witnesses claim to have seen the resurrected Jesus Christ (1 Corinthians 15:5–6). Some dismiss these witnesses' experiences as simple wish-fulfillment. That is, the followers of Jesus so desperately wanted to see their Leader again that they imagined they saw Him after His death.

However, such a theory contradicts the known facts. The actions of Christ's followers prior to and immediately after His death demonstrate that they had no expectation of His resurrection, even though Christ had predicted it many times before. Had they believed His resurrection was imminent, why would they have deserted Christ prior to His death? Why wouldn't they have camped out at the empty tomb Saturday night in anticipation of the greatest event in human history? The answer is that they were not expecting to see Christ again.

But they did. And they were so convinced of what they saw that, with the exception of the apostle John, the disciples experienced horrible martyrs' deaths. Beyond those who personally saw the resurrected Christ, there were countless others during the early decades of the Christian faith who claimed to have experienced a life-changing encounter with Jesus Christ—a claim that resulted in a great personal sacrifice:

> And others experienced mockings and scourgings, yes, also chains and imprisonment. They were stoned, they were sawn in two, they were tempted, they were put to death with the sword; they went about in sheepskins, in goatskins, being destitute, afflicted, ill-treated . . . (Hebrews 11:36–37)

More than two thousand years later millions of people around the globe are enduring persecution and death because they claim to have had a personal encounter with Jesus Christ. It is estimated that in the twentieth century alone there were 45 million Christian martyrs. A willingness to die for a claimed experience with God argues strongly for the veracity of that experience. As Pascal said, "I believe those witnesses that get their throats cut."

Other people throughout history have experienced God, not while they were searching for Him but when they were running from

Him. Although C. S. Lewis grew up in a religious home, as a young man he became resentful toward religion. Part of Lewis's disenchantment with Christianity stemmed from his conviction that the Christian belief system offered no answer to the problem of evil. By the time Lewis entered Oxford University in 1917 he was an agnostic. However, through his personal friendship with J. R. R. Tolkien and Owen Barfield, C. S. Lewis finally abandoned his agnosticism and surrendered on his knees to the belief that "God was God," becoming what he later called the "most reluctant convert in all England."[39]

In more recent times agnostic A. N. Wilson shook the intellectual community when he announced to the world on Palm Sunday, 2009, that he was renouncing atheism and returning to historic Christianity. A week later, on Easter Sunday, Wilson penned a letter explaining his rationale for his change:

> My own return to faith has surprised no one more than myself. Why did I return to it? . . . My belief has come about in large measure because of the lives and examples of people I have known— not the famous, not saints, but friends and relations who have lived, and faced death, in the light of the Resurrection story, or in the quiet acceptance that they have a future after they die.
>
> The Easter story answers their questions about spiritual aspects of humanity. It changes people's lives because it helps us understand that we, like Jesus, are born as spiritual beings. . . .
>
> But an even stronger argument is the way that Christian faith transforms individual lives—the lives of the men and women with whom you mingle on a daily basis, the man, woman or child next to you in church tomorrow morning.[40]

One of the basic principles of rationality is that how things appear from our experience is a logical reason for believing how things are, unless there is good reason to believe otherwise. That means that we should accept the testimony of an experience from another person unless there is reason not to. For example, if someone reports he witnessed a car accident, we should be inclined to believe him, unless of course, he is blind.

The experiential argument for the existence of God is not limited to one or two people but encompasses millions of people throughout history from every station of life and every nation in the world. Furthermore, millions of people have embraced belief in God in spite of ridicule, torture, and even death. Evolution provides no answer for why so many millions of people would embrace a belief that is contrary to their own self-interest.

THE CHOICE

While the atheist cannot prove there is no God, we who are believers must honestly admit that we cannot prove there is a God. Yet the bottom-line question is, does the evidence argue for or against the existence of God?

Every day we make choices based on the best available evidence rather than absolute proof. The amount of evidence we require to make a decision is determined by the importance of the decision.

For example, let's say that you prefer sweetened iced tea. If someone places two glasses of iced tea in front of you and says one is sweetened and the other is unsweetened and the host cannot remember which is which, you might be willing to take a chance and randomly select one, hoping you got the sweetened tea. After all, the consequences of selecting the wrong glass are not that grave.

However, suppose instead of adding sweetener to the tea, your host said, "A cyanide tablet accidently fell into one of the glasses, and I cannot remember which one." I would imagine you would require a lot more evidence before you chose to drink from one of the glasses.

The choice of belief or disbelief in God carries far more serious consequences than even the possibility of drinking from a poisoned glass of iced tea. As Mortimer Adler concluded, "More consequences for life and action follow from the affirmation or denial of God than from any other question."[41] It would seem only logical that before someone embraced the idea that there is no God, he would require substantial evidence to support his belief.

Instead, the argument from the universe, the complexity of the universe's design, the uniqueness of human beings, and the experiences of millions of people throughout history are strong evidences that point toward the existence of God. For the atheist to dismiss this evidence means that he must "slide into eternity with his fingers crossed," hoping he was right.[42]

Why would any rational person want to take that risk?

CHAPTER TWO

HOW CAN I KNOW THE BIBLE IS TRUE?

It's one thing to acquiesce to the claim that somewhere in the cosmos is an Intelligent Being who is responsible for the existence and complexity of the universe. However, it is a giant leap to conclude that this Being is the personal God of Abraham, Isaac, and Jacob, who implanted Himself in the womb of a teenage Jewish girl in a remote corner of the earth, was crucified to atone for the sins of the world, rose from the dead, ascended into heaven, and is returning to earth one day to establish His kingdom forever. Why couldn't that Intelligent Being be Allah of the Qur'an, the Force from *Star Wars*, or any of the thousands of other deities that have been worshipped throughout human history?

The answer is the Bible. Almost all the knowledge we have about the identity, attributes, words, commands, and desires of the God Christians worship is contained in the pages of Scripture. Of course, there are other religious books like the Qur'an and the Bhagavad Gita that also claim to be the depository of information about their respective gods. So the question is, how can we know the Bible is true?

At first glance, polls seem to indicate that the majority of Americans believe that the Bible is a sacred text. A survey by the Barna Group revealed that out of two dozen religious books listed, only one book was judged to be "sacred or holy" by at least 5 percent of the public: the Bible. Amazingly, 84 percent of respondents believed that the Bible was a sacred text (and 84 percent of those surveyed also identified themselves as Christians).[1]

However, when probed more deeply about their specific beliefs regarding the Bible, only 30 percent of those 18 to 25 years old and 39 percent of those ages 26 to 44 believe that the Bible "is totally accurate in all the principles it teaches." Furthermore, 56 percent of those ages 18 to 25 and 40 percent of those 26 to 44 believe that the Bible teaches the same spiritual truth as other sacred texts. David Kinnaman of the Barna Group, who oversaw the analysis of the research, concludes that the "central theme of young people's approach to the Bible is skepticism. They question the Bible's history as well as its relevance to their lives, leading many young people to reject the Bible as containing everything one needs to live a meaningful life."[2]

It is understandable why a growing number of young adults doubt the veracity of the Bible. They are regularly bombarded by attacks on the integrity of the Scriptures from professors in both secular and Christian universities, movies, and best-selling books. One of the main characters in Dan Brown's bestseller *The Da Vinci Code*, Sir Leigh Teabing, articulates the conventional wisdom about the Bible among secularists: "The Bible is a product of man, my dear. Not of God. The Bible did not fall magically from the clouds. Man created it as a historical record of tumultuous times, and it has evolved through countless translations, additions, and revisions. History has never had a definitive version of the book."[3]

Unfortunately, such a low view of the Bible is becoming increasingly embraced by Christians, with devastating results. When I was a freshman in high school, I felt God's clear calling to become a pastor. I began to read the Bible and every book about the Bible I could get my hands on. I shared my faith regularly with everyone I could. I organized evangelistic projects at my public high school to attempt to introduce my classmates to Christ. I arose early every morning to travel to a local park before school to pray and read my worn-out green hardback *Living Bible*. I fell asleep every night listening to recorded sermons by great preachers. I read entire books of the New Testament.

Then I went to college. The Christian university I attended required taking religion classes taught by professors from a variety of theological perspectives. I took a class from the chairman of the religion department, who was an excellent teacher. However, he regularly challenged the belief I had been taught in my church that every verse in the Bible was inspired by God and contained no errors of any kind. My professor made such pronouncements as:

- "No intelligent scholar believes Moses wrote the first five books of the Bible."
- "The Bible is a collection of men's thoughts about God. The Old Testament represents man's lowest estimation of who God is—a cruel, bloodthirsty deity. The New Testament represents man's highest idea of God."
- "God did not command Joshua to kill every living being in Ai and Jericho, as the Bible records. Instead, that is what Joshua thought God commanded because of Joshua's low estimation of God."
- "Moses and the Israelites were not supernaturally led through the Red Sea but through the Reed Sea, which was only a few inches deep." (If that's true, that's even a greater miracle because it means all those Egyptians drowned in just a few inches of water!)

A steady diet of those kinds of stinging indictments against the trustworthiness of Scripture began to affect my spiritual life. I read the Bible less frequently and gave up my intensive program of Scripture memory. After all, why spend hours reading and memorizing words that may or may not be true? I was less enthusiastic about sharing my faith with others. How did I know the message I was sharing was really from God? Within a few months, I began questioning whether I wanted to go into the ministry. Why devote my life to preaching from a book that is filled with myths, contradictions, and errors? My crisis of faith forced me to investigate for myself whether or not the Bible could be trusted as God's authoritative Word.

The issue of whether or not the Bible is true is not some secondary issue for theologians to debate but one that has serious ramifications for life and eternity. If the Bible cannot be trusted to record accurately whether Moses crossed the Red or the Reed Sea, how can we know that the Bible accurately records historical events like the virgin birth of Christ, His crucifixion, and His resurrection from the dead? If God really did not tell Joshua to kill every living thing in Jericho, how can we know that Jesus really said, "I am the way, and the truth, and the life; no one comes to the Father, but through Me" (John 14:6)? My predecessor Dr. W. A. Criswell used to refer to the "leopard theory of biblical inspiration," which says, "The Bible is inspired in spots, and I'm inspired to spot the spots!" The weakness to such an approach to the Bible is self-evident. Either all of the Bible is true or all of the Bible is suspect.

Maybe you have encountered individuals who question whether the Bible is without any error, and you are not sure how to respond to their challenges. Perhaps you have your own questions about the Bible that you have been hesitant to ask, such as:

- What real proof is there outside the Bible itself that the events it records actually happened?
- How is the Bible different than other religious books that make fantastic claims regarding the supernatural?
- What about all of the errors and contradictions in the Bible?
- How do we know that the right books actually made it into the Bible?

WHAT DO WE MEAN BY "TRUE"?

Often theologians use the word *inspired* (a term the apostle Paul also employed to describe Scripture) to describe the uniqueness of the Bible. However, couldn't one also say that the words of Shakespeare and the music of Beethoven are "inspired"? Other people use the term *inerrant* to describe the Bible, meaning that the Bible is "without error." Yet Numbers 25:9 records that twenty-four thousand Israelites died from a plague, while 1 Corinthians 10:8 says that twenty-three thousand died from the same plague. It *appears* someone made an error.

There are two key words we need to understand when it comes to the truthfulness of the Bible: *inerrancy* and *inspiration*.

Inerrancy

The word *inerrancy* refers to the quality of the final product found in the Bible. I like the way my friend and former seminary professor Dr. Charles Ryrie summarizes the concept of inerrancy: "The Bible tells the truth." Dr. Ryrie goes on to explain that "truth" can and does include "approximations, free quotations, language of appearances, and different accounts of the same event as long as those do not contradict."[4] Simply put, the inerrancy of the Bible means there is no untruth in the Bible. The apostle Paul declared,

All Scripture is inspired [literally, "God-breathed"] by God and profitable for teaching, for reproof, for correction, for training in righteousness; so that the man of God may be adequate, equipped for every good work. (2 Timothy 3:16–17)

If God is true (Romans 3:4), and Scripture is God-breathed (2 Timothy 3:16), then it logically follows that Scripture is true as well.

Inspiration

The term *inspiration* explains the process by which God communicated His message through human beings into the written words found in the Bible without any error. "How could imperfect men be expected to produce a perfect Bible?" skeptics often ask. The apostle Peter answers that question:

> For no prophecy [of Scripture] was ever made by an act of human will, but men moved by the Holy Spirit spoke from God. (2 Peter 1:21)

It is important that we claim no more and no less than the Bible claims for itself when it comes to the subjects of inerrancy and inspiration. Contrary to the assertion in *The Da Vinci Code*, the biblical writers never claim that Scripture fell magically from the clouds. Nor do they deny the human element involved in the process of recording God's message. Of all of the definitions of *inspiration* I have read, Dr. Ryrie offers the simplest and yet most complete explanation of the process of inspiration that led to the product of an inerrant Bible:

> Inspiration is God's superintending of human authors so that, using their own individual personalities, they composed and recorded without error in the words of the original autographs His revelation to man.[5]

Let's look at each of these phrases to understand exactly what we mean by inspiration and inerrancy:

"*God's superintending of human authors.*" God oversaw the whole process of inspiration. His guiding hand prevented the biblical authors from making mistakes when they penned the words in our Bible. That doesn't mean that Moses, David, Paul, Peter, and the other writers never made a mistake in anything they ever said or wrote. But when they were writing God's message, they were protected from error. For example, there are times I have spoken and written words that were untrue. But that doesn't mean that everything I've ever spoken or written is untrue. In the same way, the biblical authors were fallible men who, through God's protective power, produced an infallible Bible.

"*Their own individual personalities.*" While God originated the message found in every word of the Bible, He poured that message through the individual personalities of the authors He chose. He used the emotional outbursts of King David, the angry rebukes of Moses, the skepticism of Solomon, and the systematic reasoning of Paul to deliver His message. Theologians refer to this phenomenon as "dual authorship." God used a variety of people in different circumstances to produce His message without any error. This explains why there is both diversity of style and yet unity of message in the Bible. God used a variety of people to produce one message.

"*They composed and recorded.*" Some of the Bible contains God's direct dictation such as the Ten Commandments found in Exodus 20 or God's message to the seven churches found in Revelation 2–3, in which God basically said to the apostle John, "Get a pen and a piece of papyrus and write these words . . ."

However, most of the Bible was composed rather than recorded. For example, when David pleaded with God, "Be gracious to me, O God, according to Your lovingkindness" in Psalm 51:1, David was not recording God's message word for word ("God, should I put a comma after 'me'?"). No, this psalm represents a heartfelt cry from David, pleading for God's mercy. Yet it is still part of God's message for us today.

"*Without error.*" As previously discussed, this phrase simply means that the Bible tells the truth in all of its words. The Scripture is truth without any mixture of error.

"*In the words of the original autographs.*" The terms *inspiration* and *inerrancy* only apply to the original manuscripts (or "autographs") of the writings of the biblical writers. We no longer have those original manuscripts but thousands of copies that have been produced from those lost originals. We will discuss later in this chapter the amazing accuracy of those copies, but the question for now is, does a belief in the inspiration and inerrancy of Scripture really matter if it only applies to original manuscripts that no longer exist? It does, and here's why.

Suppose you have a fifty-dollar bill in your purse or wallet that was produced from engraving plates at the US Treasury. Those plates (the "originals") were made according to the exact specifications of the government. You have never seen those engraving plates and never will. In fact, those engraving plates may have been destroyed by now. But even though the original plates are not available, doesn't it make a difference whether those original plates were legitimate or counterfeit plates? The authenticity of the fifty-dollar bill depends upon the authenticity of the original plates.

So it is with the Bible. The fact that we do not have the original manuscripts does not diminish the importance of whether those manuscripts were the authentic Word of God. If the original manuscripts of God's Word were filled with myths and errors, so is the Bible you hold in your hand today. While an inspired and inerrant original doesn't *necessarily* guarantee inspired and inerrant copies, an uninspired and errant original will *always* result in an uninspired and errant copy.

"*His revelation to man.*" Does the Bible contain any lies? Of course, it does! Genesis 3:4 records Satan's lie to Eve about the consequences of eating the forbidden fruit: "You shall not die!" As Dr. Ryrie explains, the phrase "His revelation" has to be broad enough to include Satan's lies, biblical writers' research (Luke's gospel was the result of research rather than firsthand experience), emotional outbursts (Romans 9:1–2), quotations from nonbiblical sources (Titus 1:12), approximations, paraphrases of Scripture (such as those used by the writer of Hebrews), and the language of appearance (such as "the four corners of the earth" in Isaiah 11:12).

HISTORY SPEAKS

Some argue that belief in a Bible without error is a recent development in Christianity that reflects a larger (and temporary) societal shift toward conservatism. However, the concept of an inerrant Bible has always been part of the Christian movement. Consider the statements of some of Christianity's most respected leaders:

- Irenaeus, speaking for the ancient Greek Church, wrote, "The Scriptures are indeed perfect, since they were spoken by the Word of God and His spirit."[6]
- Augustine, representing the Western Church, expressed the same sentiment: "As to the other writings . . . I do not accept their teaching as true on the mere ground of the opinion held by them; but . . . the canonical writings are free from error."[7]
- Martin Luther, the leader of the Protestant Reformation, declared that the "Holy Scriptures cannot err."[8]
- John Calvin believed that the Bible was "the pure word of God" and was "the infallible rule of His holy truth."[9]
- John Wesley, evangelist and founder of Methodism, defied the current thinking of his day that doubted the truthfulness of the Bible by concluding, "If there be any mistakes in the Bible, there may as well be a thousand. If there be one falsehood in that book, it did not come from the God of truth."[10]

Kirsopp Lake, a liberal professor at Harvard University, admitted that it is liberals, not conservatives, who have departed from the historical understanding of the nature of Scripture. "How many were there, for instance, in Christian churches in the eighteenth century who doubted the infallible inspiration of all Scripture? A few, perhaps, but very few. . . . It is we [liberals] who have departed from the tradition. . . . The Bible and the *corpus theologicum* of the church are on the fundamentalist side."[11]

The testimony of these early church fathers and leaders is compelling, but certainly not conclusive. People have been wrong throughout history in their beliefs about everything from the earth's orbit around the sun to the existence of germs. How can we know that Christianity's past leaders were not similarly mistaken in their beliefs about the Bible?

EVIDENCES FOR THE TRUSTWORTHINESS OF THE BIBLE

There is no way to prove that the Bible is God's inspired and inerrant Word, any more than we can prove that God exists. However, we can remove a few potholes in the road to belief. In the remainder of this chapter we are going to look at the five greatest evidences for the inerrancy of the Bible and answer three of the most common objections to the belief that the Bible is God's inspired and exclusive message to us.

Evidence #1: The Bible's Claims about Itself

Those who doubt the deity of Jesus Christ often say that Jesus Himself never claimed to be God. Instead, some overzealous followers invented the myth that Jesus was the Son of God to make a good story even better! Some people make a similar argument about the Bible: "The Bible never claims to be the inerrant, inspired Word of God. Instead, rabid religious fundamentalists are making such assertions." Yet consider what both the Old and New Testaments claim about themselves.

Old Testament. Hundreds of times in the Old Testament you find the phrase "The Lord said" or something similar. For example . . .

"Then God spoke all these words saying . . ." (Exodus 20:1)

"Listen, O heavens, and hear, O earth; for the Lᴏʀᴅ speaks . . ." (Isaiah 1:2)

"The words of Jeremiah . . . to whom the word of the Lᴏʀᴅ came." (Jeremiah 1:1–2)

In Psalm 95 we read these words: "Today, if you would hear His voice, do not harden your hearts, as at Meribah, as in the day of Massah in the wilderness" (vv. 7–8). Honestly, we do not know the name of the human author who composed this psalm. But nearly a thousand years later the writer of Hebrews in the New Testament identified the author of this psalm as the Holy Spirit of God:

Therefore, just as *the Holy Spirit* says, "Tᴏᴅᴀʏ ɪғ ʏᴏᴜ ʜᴇᴀʀ Hɪs ᴠᴏɪᴄᴇ . . ." (Hebrews 3:7)

When the apostle Paul declares that "all Scripture is inspired by God" he is referring primarily (but not exclusively as we will see) to the Old Testament. Paul described every word of the Old Testament as "God-breathed" (2 Timothy 3:16 ɴɪᴠ). The apostle Peter was also primarily referring to the Old Testament when he explained that "men moved by the Holy Spirit spoke from God" (2 Peter 1:21).

Jesus Christ also believed in the inspiration and inerrancy of the Old Testament. As we will see in the next section, during Jesus' early ministry the Old Testament was already in written form and included the same books that are in our Old Testament today. It almost seems that Jesus went out of the way to put His stamp of approval on those stories in the Old Testament that are routinely labeled as myth by liberal scholars.

For example, today many people doubt the claim in Genesis that the entire human race can be traced back to a first man and woman. But Jesus quoted from that account in explaining God's blueprint for marriage:

And He answered and said, "Have you not read that He who created them from the beginning MADE THEM MALE AND FEMALE, and said, 'FOR THIS REASON A MAN SHALL LEAVE HIS FATHER AND MOTHER AND BE JOINED TO HIS WIFE, AND THE TWO SHALL BECOME ONE FLESH'?" (Matthew 19:4–5)

Some people find it difficult to accept the story of Jonah being swallowed by a great fish. Yet Jesus not only embraced that story but used it as an illustration of His coming resurrection from the dead:

But He answered and said to them, "An evil and adulterous generation craves for a sign; and yet no sign shall be given to it but the sign of Jonah the prophet; for just as JONAH WAS THREE DAYS AND THREE NIGHTS IN THE BELLY OF THE SEA MONSTER, so will the Son of Man be three days and three nights in the heart of the earth." (Matthew 12:39–40)

Other people scoff at the notion of a man named Noah constructing an ark large enough to save himself, his family, and representatives of all animal life from a universal flood. Yet Jesus linked the historicity of that event in the Old Testament with the certainty of His second coming:

For the coming of the Son of Man will be just like the days of Noah. For as in those days before the flood they were eating and drinking, marrying and giving in marriage, until the day that Noah entered the ark, and they did not understand until the flood came and took them all away; so will the coming of the Son of Man be. (Matthew 24:37–39)

Jesus believed in a historical person named Noah who built an actual ark to protect him from a very real flood that swept away the entire human race. Notice Jesus' concluding phrase: ". . . so will the coming of the Son of Man be." If the story of Noah and the great flood is a myth, then the second coming of Christ is also a myth. Jesus' words do not allow for a fictional flood and a literal second coming.

Jesus' belief in the inspiration and inerrancy of the Old Testament extends beyond some of the better known stories and includes every single word used in Scripture. For example, consider Jesus' teaching about the reality of life after death. Jesus used the Old Testament to rebut the claims of the Jewish sect of the Sadducees for their disbelief in the resurrection of the dead. Jesus referred them to Exodus 3:6, which records God's words to Moses at the burning bush:

> But regarding the resurrection of the dead, have you not read what was spoken to you by God: "I AM THE GOD OF ABRAHAM, AND THE GOD OF ISAAC, AND THE GOD OF JACOB"? He is not the God of the dead but of the living. (Matthew 22:31–32)

Abraham, Isaac, and Jacob had been dead for hundreds of years prior to God's conversation with Moses. The most common way to refer to the dearly departed is in the past tense. One would have expected God to identify Himself to Moses by saying, "I *was* the God of Abraham, Isaac, and Jacob." But since the patriarchs were still alive in heaven hundreds of years after their death, God declares, "I *am* the God of Abraham, Isaac, and Jacob." Jesus based His whole argument for the reality of life after death on the use of the present tense instead of the past tense of a single word of the Old Testament!

Jesus' confidence in the truthfulness of the Old Testament extends beyond stories and individual words to include even the letters and strokes that make up each word:

Do not think that I came to abolish the Law or the Prophets; I did not come to abolish but to fulfill. For truly I say to you, until heaven and earth pass away, not the smallest letter or stroke shall pass away from the Law until all is accomplished. (Matthew 5:17–18)

The smallest letter in the Hebrew language is the letter *yodh*, which is approximately the size of an apostrophe in English. Jesus is claiming that every letter in every word of the Hebrew Old Testament has a purpose behind it that is to be fulfilled, and therefore, every letter in every word is inspired by God.

Letters in a word can make a big difference in the meaning of that word. For example, imagine you have your money deposited in a bank and you ask a knowledgeable friend about the condition of that bank. Your friend texts you, "That bank is through!" Alarmed, you withdraw all of your assets as quickly as you can. Several days later you thank him for the warning only to discover that his autocorrect had accidentally changed the last word of his sentence. He meant to write, "That bank is tough!" The difference between *through* and *tough* is only two letters, but the meanings and applications are vastly different. Jesus said every single letter of the Old Testament can be trusted.

The Lord's concept of inerrancy also includes the smallest "stroke." The only difference between some letters in the Hebrew alphabet is a small stroke (referred to as a "tittle" in the King James Version) that can only be seen by careful examination. In fact, when I took Hebrew in seminary many years ago, students actually brought magnifying glasses to class so they could identify certain letters by the presence or absence of such strokes! For example, consider the English words *rat* and *fat*. The difference between the two very different words is just a single stroke. Insert a tiny, horizontal stroke on the "r" and you have an "f" and a completely different word and meaning in a sentence. Jesus' belief in the inspiration of the Old Testament extended to the smallest letter of a word and the minutest strokes found on the letters that comprise those words.

New Testament. What about the inspiration and inerrancy of the New Testament? There are many historical, archaeological, and bibliological reasons to trust the New Testament, as we will discover later. But do the New Testament writers claim the same degree of inspiration for their own writings as they do for the Old Testament? It surprises many people to learn that the New Testament writers actually labeled some of their contemporaries' works as "Scripture." For example, Paul uses both the Old and New Testaments to defend his instruction to pay generously those who work at preaching (one reason Paul has always been my favorite apostle!):

> For the Scripture says, "YOU SHALL NOT MUZZLE THE OX WHILE HE IS THRESH-ING," and "The laborer is worthy of his wages." (1 Timothy 5:18)

The first scripture Paul quotes is Deuteronomy 25:4, in which God commanded the Israelites to allow their oxen to enjoy some of the grain they were working hard to separate from the stalk by dragging a large stone across the threshing floor. Paul finds a timeless principle from that command in the Old Testament that applies to pastors who are diligent in their work: they should be generously compensated for their efforts. But then Paul quotes another scripture: "The laborer is worthy of his wages" (1 Timothy 5:18).

Honestly, I have read that passage for many years and assumed it was also a quotation from the Old Testament. However, that command actually comes from Luke 10:7, in the New Testament. Jesus was instructing His advance team before sending them throughout Israel to announce His upcoming appearances:

Stay in that house, eating and drinking what they give you; for the laborer is worthy of his wages.

Luke's gospel had been completed a few years prior to Paul's letter to Timothy but was considered by Paul to be just as authoritative as the book of Deuteronomy in the Old Testament. He describes both as "Scripture."

In one of the seminaries I attended a professor claimed that the writings of Paul did not have the same authority as the words of Jesus Christ. Instead, he said that many of Paul's writings (especially about the role of women in the church) were the musings of a bitter, old bachelor who hated women, we were told. Yet the apostle Peter held a different view about Paul's writings. In describing God's patience toward delaying His judgment, Peter writes:

And regard the patience of our Lord as salvation; just as also our beloved brother Paul, according to the wisdom given him, wrote to you, as also in all his letters, speaking in them of these things, in which are some things hard to understand, which the untaught and unstable distort, as they do also *the rest of the Scriptures*, to their own destruction. (2 Peter 3:15–16)

Even Peter, leader of the church at Jerusalem, found some of Paul's writings difficult to decipher. Nevertheless, Peter referred to Paul's writings as an authoritative source to support his own argument. Even more significantly, Peter included Paul's writings in the category of "the Scriptures."

Some would argue that to use the Bible's claims about itself as evidence for its trustworthiness is to engage in circular reasoning: "The Bible is true because the Bible says it is true." Maybe the Bible's self-claims of inspiration and inerrancy are like the hyperbolic blurbs found on the jackets of many books: "Best Book Ever Written!" or "The Most Provocative Piece of Literature Ever Penned."

Admittedly, the Bible's claims about itself is perhaps the weakest of all the evidence for its trustworthiness. Nevertheless, it is important to realize that when we declare that the Bible is God-breathed and free from error we are not claiming more about the Bible than Jesus, the apostles, or the biblical writers claimed about the Scriptures.

Evidence #2: Fulfilled Prophecy

One of the strongest arguments for the credibility of the Bible is the amazing number of fulfilled prophecies one finds in Scripture. Detailed predictions about specific individuals, nations, and events were foretold hundreds of years before they occurred, and their fulfillments have been historically verified. It is important to note that no other religious books such as the Qur'an, the Analects of Confucius, or the Book of Mormon contain specific prophecies that can be independently confirmed, yet hundreds of such prophecies can be found in the Bible. Allow me to cite just two examples.

In about 700 BC the Old Testament prophet Isaiah predicted that the nation of Babylon—a relatively minor player on the world scene at the time—would conquer Judah and take her captive:

> Then Isaiah said to Hezekiah, "Hear the word of the LORD of hosts, 'Behold, the days are coming when all that is in your house and all that your fathers have laid up in store to this day will be carried to Babylon; nothing will be left,' says the LORD." (Isaiah 39:5–6)

Isaiah's prediction came true more than one hundred years later in 586 BC, when Babylon ultimately prevailed over Judah. Perhaps Isaiah just got lucky. After all, even a broken clock is right twice a day! But Isaiah's remarkable prophecies did not stop there.

Isaiah looked beyond Judah's defeat by Babylon and predicted that Babylon itself would be conquered by another nation (Isaiah 21:9). This specific prophecy was fulfilled in 539 BC, nearly 150 years after Isaiah made this prophecy. But Isaiah had an even more amazing prediction to make. The prophet identified by name the king who would allow Judah to return from her exile in Babylon to rebuild Jerusalem:

> It is I who says of Cyrus, "He is My shepherd! And he will perform all My desire." And he declares of Jerusalem, "She will be built." And of the temple, "Your foundation will be laid." (Isaiah 44:28)

History tells us that Cyrus, king of Persia, did conquer Babylon in 539 BC, and in March of 538 BC King Cyrus decreed that the Israelites could return to their homeland. Remember, Isaiah predicted all of this about 150 years earlier! This prophecy is not a general prediction about a vague event involving an unidentified individual. Instead, this is a specific prediction concerning the defeat of one nation by another nation, the subsequent defeat of that nation by yet another nation, and the leader of that nation—identified by name—who would issue a specific order allowing the rebuilding of the originally mentioned nation. Isaiah referred to Cyrus as the king of Persia, one hundred years before Cyrus was even born!

Let me illustrate how astounding such a prophecy is. Suppose that in 1850 someone predicted that one day America would be attacked by terrorists on its own soil. Furthermore, after that attack, the president of the United States would order the invasion of the country of Iraq. And the name of that United States president would be George W. Bush. What are the chances of someone accurately predicting in 1850 the actions of a named president who would not even be born for another one hundred years?

When we turn to the New Testament we find even more amazing examples of fulfilled prophecies, all centered on Jesus Christ. There are at least sixty-one major prophecies in the Old Testament concerning the expected Messiah that were fulfilled by Jesus Christ. A skeptic might argue, "Perhaps Jesus, acquainted with these Old Testament prophecies, purposefully tried to fulfill these predictions in order to appear to be the Messiah."

Frankly, some of the prophecies about Messiah (such as the words He would speak on the cross) could be explained that way. But there are other Old Testament prophecies about the Messiah—made hundreds of years before the fact—over which Jesus had no control: the place of His birth (Micah 5:2), the time of His birth (Daniel 9:25), the manner of His birth (Isaiah 7:14), His betrayal for thirty pieces of silver (Zechariah 11:12), the manner of His death (Psalm 22:16), the people's reaction to His death (Psalm 22:7–8), and His burial in a rich man's tomb (Isaiah 53:9).

According to one mathematician, the chances of one man in history fulfilling just eight of those specific prophecies is 1 in 10^{17}. In other words, that would be 1 in 100,000,000,000,000,000. To illustrate the high degree of improbability such a figure represents, imagine taking 10^{17} silver coins and spreading them over the entire state of Texas. This amount of silver coins would cover the entire state two feet deep. Then, take one of those 10^{17} coins and mark it with a black X and throw it back into the pile. After you have thoroughly mixed up all of the coins, blindfold a man and allow him to walk all over the state and then randomly pick up one of those silver coins. What are the chances that the coin he selects is the one with the black X on it? One in 10^{17}—the same chance that Jesus Christ could have randomly fulfilled eight of the sixty-one Old Testament prophecies about His life. These are just two examples of the dozens of fulfilled prophecies that affirm the divine origin of the Bible.[12]

Evidence #3: The Unity of the Bible

Contrast the origin of the Bible with two other well-known religious books. Muslims believe that the Qur'an is God's final revelation to man. They claim that over a period of twenty-three years (AD 610–632), Allah dispatched the angel Gabriel to Muhammad to reveal deep spiritual truths. Yet, in spite of having a single author, there is an amazing lack of unity in the Qur'an. Ken Woodward, writing in *Newsweek*, contrasts the Qur'an with the Bible: "As sacred texts, however, the Bible and the Qur'an could not be more different. To read the Qur'an is like entering a stream. At almost any point one may come upon a command of God, a burst of prayer, a theological pronouncement, the story of an earlier prophet or a description of a final judgment. . . . None of its 114 suras, or chapters, focuses on a single theme."[13]

According to Joseph Smith, the founder of The Church of Jesus Christ of Latter-day Saints (commonly known as LDS or the Mormon Church), an angel named Moroni appeared to him in 1823 near his home in Manchester, New York, and showed him golden plates containing new information about Jesus Christ. Four years later, the angel gave Smith the golden plates to translate into English. Those golden plates became the Book of Mormon, which Smith published in 1830 (after he conveniently returned the plates back to the angel). Yet in spite of its claims of divine revelation, the Book of Mormon does not contain historically verifiable facts or fulfilled prophecies.

Unlike the Qur'an and the Book of Mormon, which were each penned by a single individual over a short period of time, the Bible was written by as many as forty authors over a span of fifteen hundred years. Moses was the first named author and began writing around 1440 BC, while John wrote the last book of the Bible around AD 100.

The men who composed and recorded God's message were very diverse. Moses was a political leader, David was a shepherd, Solomon was a monarch, Daniel was a prime minister, Amos was a herdsman, Luke was a doctor, Paul was a rabbi, and Peter was a fisherman. In addition to having a diversity of authors, the Bible was composed in a variety of locations that spanned more than two thousand miles from Babylon to Jerusalem and Rome. The Scriptures were written in a variety of settings including deserts, cities, and dungeons.

Arthur Pink observes, "Yet, despite these varying circumstances, conditions, and workmen, the Bible is one book, behind its many parts there is an unmistakable organic unity. It contains one system of doctrine, one code of ethics, one plan of salvation, and one rule of faith."[14] For example, consider the unity of theme in the Bible. Genesis begins with a description of mankind's fall and need for redemption—a redemption that is accomplished in the Gospels and fully realized in the book of Revelation.

There is also a unity of symbolism in the Bible that is consistent in both the Old and New Testaments: fire represents judgment, water and oil symbolize the Holy Spirit, and blood is the agent of redemption. The only explanation for such unity in a book that was composed under such diverse circumstances is that there was a divine Author who oversaw the final product. My friend Erwin Lutzer vividly illustrates why the unity of the Bible is such a convincing argument for its divine origin:

> Imagine various pieces of a cathedral arriving from different countries and cities, converging on a central location. In fact, imagine that investigation proves that forty different sculptors made contributions over a period of many centuries. Yet the pieces fit together to form a single magnificent structure. Would this not be proof that behind the project was a single mind, one designer who used His workmen to sculpt a well-conceived plan? The Bible is that cathedral, assembled by one super-intelligent architect.[15]

Evidence #4: Early Acceptance of the Message

One of the strongest arguments for the veracity of the Bible—especially the New Testament—is the degree to which its message was quickly and fully embraced by the early followers of Christianity. One of the standard arguments liberals used to use in casting doubt about the authenticity of the New Testament was that it was written many decades after the life of Jesus and was, therefore, subject to great embellishments like the miracles and the resurrection. As the years passed, the theory goes, some of Jesus' followers added fictitious events like the miracles and the resurrection to the story of Jesus' life to make Christianity more appealing to potential converts. Obviously, the longer the interval between a person's life and the written record of that life, the greater the chance for myth to be added to the story.

However, even liberal scholars like John A. T. Robinson now accept that the majority of the New Testament was written between AD 40 and 65, making the addition of fictitious events highly unlikely. For example, suppose a book was published today that said three days after President Ronald Reagan's funeral on June 11, 2004, he arose from his grave in Simi Valley and was seen by over five hundred people in Southern California, naming some of those individuals who claimed to have seen a resurrected Reagan. The book would not last beyond one printing because its credibility would be destroyed by those who were alive and knew better. Such a book could only gain traction once everyone who was living at the time of Reagan's death had died and, therefore, could not dispute the story. Similarly, the fact that the New Testament was written within a few years of the events it reports—and was accepted as fact—is great evidence for its authenticity.

Furthermore, consider the extent to which the New Testament writers—the majority of whom were devout Jews—replaced the basic tenets of Judaism with new beliefs. They abandoned the sacrificial system that had been in place for fourteen hundred years, they changed their day of worship from the Sabbath to the first day of the week, they replaced the sign of faith from circumcision to baptism, and they relegated the Mosaic Law to nothing more than a shadow of the newer revelation from Jesus Christ (Colossians 2:17).

This dramatic shift in beliefs and practices was not limited to the New Testament writers. Almost overnight, thousands of Jews in Jerusalem radically altered their most cherished spiritual convictions and embraced an entirely new spiritual paradigm. Author J. P. Moreland explains just how momentous such a shift was:

> [The Jewish people] believed that these institutions were entrusted to them by God. They believed that to abandon these institutions would be to risk their souls being damned to hell after death.
>
> Now a rabbi named Jesus appears from a lower-class region. He teaches for three years, gathers a following of lower- and middle-class people, gets in trouble with the authorities, and gets crucified along with thirty thousand other Jewish men who are executed during this time period.
>
> But five weeks after he's crucified, over ten thousand Jews are following him and claiming that he is the initiator of a new religion. And get this: they're willing to give up or alter all five of the social institutions that they have been taught since childhood, and have such importance both sociologically and theologically. . . . Something very big was going on.[16]

That "something very big" was the resurrection of Jesus Christ from the dead. News of Christ's empty tomb spread like wildfire throughout Jerusalem. Remember, the Jewish leaders were so fearful that the disciples might steal Jesus' body and claim that He had fulfilled His prophecy of a resurrection that they begged Pontius Pilate for a Roman guard unit to secure the tomb:

Sir, we remember that when He was still alive that deceiver said, "After three days I am to rise again." Therefore, give orders for the grave to be made secure until the third day, otherwise His disciples may come and steal Him away and say to the people, "He has risen from the dead," and the last deception will be worse than the first. (Matthew 27:63–64)

The implausibility of the eleven remaining disciples overpowering an entire Roman guard unit (Matthew 28:11 indicates there were multiple guards securing the tomb) is evident, especially given the fact that their leader, Peter, had deserted Christ to save his own life. But an even more compelling argument against the disciples-stole-the-body theory is the behavior of the disciples after the alleged resurrection.

If indeed the disciples had been able to subdue the powerful guard unit and abscond with Jesus' body (which they could have done much more easily on Friday evening before He was placed in the tomb and the guard unit was posted), then they were part of the greatest cover-up in history. While it is true that religious zealots throughout history have died for false beliefs they thought were true, no rational person would die for a belief he knew was a lie.

Many years ago I had the privilege of hosting the late Charles Colson at the church I was serving, only a few years after the notorious Watergate scandal that had ended the Nixon presidency in disgrace. When Colson spoke to our church he noted that he and the other White House conspirators had been able cover to up the truth about the break-in at Democratic headquarters only for two weeks until John Dean, one of the president's counselors, turned state's evidence in order to protect himself. Cover-ups are eventually uncovered.

By contrast, the disciples were willing to endure imprisonment, torture, and ultimately death rather than recant their testimony that they had seen Jesus Christ in His resurrected body. Surely, one of those eleven would have broken under such pressure and revealed the truth had the disciples conspired to perpetrate a myth. Instead, the disciples maintained their story until the very end—a story that could have easily been dismissed if either the Jews or the Romans had been able to produce the body of Jesus Christ. Yet the reality of Christ's resurrection was so quickly embraced by so many that in less than three hundred years the faith of these eleven men effectively toppled the Roman Empire.

Evidence#5: Archaeological Evidence

Is there any independent confirmation for the historical reliability of the Scriptures outside of the Bible? It is important to understand that archaeology can never prove that the Bible is true for two reasons. First, the archaeological record is limited in *size*. One would have to find independent confirmation for every event recorded in the sixty-six books of the Bible in order for archaeology to verify the authenticity of Scripture. No one expects that to happen.

Furthermore, the archaeological record is limited in *scope*. For example, suppose the remains of the wall of Jericho were discovered, confirming that such a wall existed and collapsed suddenly as Joshua 6 indicates. However, such a discovery could never prove that God was the One who caused the wall to crumble.

Nevertheless, the plethora of locations, names, and events that have been confirmed by external sources—especially in contrast to religious books such as the Qur'an and the Book of Mormon—provides a strong argument for the truthfulness of the Bible. For example, discoveries that relate to the Old Testament include clay tablets discovered at Ebla in Northern Syria that date back to 2300 BC and mention the existence of a number of cities in the Old Testament, including Sodom and Gomorrah. There is evidence of earthquake activity in that area, along with large amounts of bituminous pitch that could explain the "fire and brimstone" that destroyed those cities.

Excavations of the city of Jericho from 1930-1936 reveal not only the existence of the city but evidence supporting the sudden collapse of the wall encompassing the city. One of those men on the archeological team writes, "As to the main fact, then, there remains no doubt: the walls fell outwards so completely that the attackers would be able to clamber up and over their ruins into the city. Why so unusual? Because the walls of cities do not fall outwards, they fall inwards. And yet in Joshua 6:20 we read, 'The wall fell down flat. Then the people went up into the city, every man straight before him, and they took the city.' The walls were made to fall outward."[17]

The Old Testament book of Daniel has come under more attacks than any other book of the Old Testament. For many years, critics argued that the name Ashpenaz mentioned in Daniel 1:3 as the chief of his officials is found nowhere in the extensive writings uncovered from ancient Babylon. Yet, a few decades ago a brick was discovered in the ruins of Babylon with the name Asphenaz on it and this brick can now be viewed in the British Museum.

For many years liberal critics of the Bible claimed that the absence of any external confirmation of a tribe known as the Hittites in the Old Testament proved that the Old Testament writers simply invented the name. However, in 1911 thousands of clay tablets confirming the existence of the Hittites were unearthed at the site of the Hittite capital.

King David is a central character in the Old Testament and his dynasty ultimately included the Messiah. However, there had not been any external historical confirmation of the existence of a king named David, much less a powerful dynasty in Israel bearing his name. All of that changed with an amazing discovery in 1994, described by Avaraham Biran:

A remarkable inscription from the ninth century BCE that refers to both the [House of David], and to the [King of Israel]. This is the first time that the name of David has been found in any ancient inscription outside of the Bible. That the inscription refers not simply to a [David] but to the house of David, the dynasty of the great Israelite king, is even more remarkable . . . this may be the oldest extra-biblical reference to Israel in Semitic script. If this inscription proves anything, it shows that both Israel and Judah, contrary to the claims of some scholarly biblical minimizers, were important kingdoms at this time.[18]

Important archaeological discoveries have also verified many names, locations, and events in the New Testament:

Luke's gospel contains numerous references to names and locations. In fact, when noted archaeologist Sir William Ramsay attempted to prove that the book of Acts (which is also attributed to Luke) contained numerous errors, he came to the conclusion that "Luke's history is unsurpassed in respect of its trustworthiness."[19]

Critics of Luke's gospel had argued that there was no empire-wide census at the time of Christ's birth, that there was no evidence of people returning to their hometowns to be registered for the purpose of taxation, and that Quirinius was not the Syrian governor. Yet recent archaeological discoveries have confirmed that the Romans conducted regular censuses, that it was customary for people living away from their homes to return for the purpose of enrolling for taxation, and that Quirinius was governor of Syria at two different times in history.

Archaeology has also confirmed many events in the book of Acts, also penned by Luke. He correctly referred to established provinces of the time (Acts 15:41, 16:2), he referred to different officers by their correct titles (Acts 13:7, 16:20), and he accurately described events such as the famine during the days of Claudius Caesar (Acts 11:28). Dr. Clifford Wilson concludes, "[Luke] was an eyewitness of so much that is recorded in the Acts, and the source documents have now been recognized as first-class historical writings."[20]

John 5:2 describes a pool with five porticoes in Jerusalem called Bethesda. For centuries, many critics of the Bible doubted such a pool existed. But in 1871 French architect C. Mauss discovered a cistern while restoring an old church in the northeast quarter of Jerusalem. Later excavations confirmed the existence of two pools large enough to hold a large number of people.

In 1990 a tomb was discovered in Jerusalem verifying that a man named Caiaphas was the high priest in Jerusalem at the time of Christ's death, just as the Bible describes.

In 1961 Italian archaeologist Antonio Frova discovered an inscription on a stone slab in Caesarea naming Pontius Pilate as a Roman governor, as described in Matthew 27:2 and Luke 3:1.

Inscriptions discovered in the ancient city of Corinth refer to a meat market that Paul describes in 1 Corinthians 10:25.

The great theater in Ephesus described by Luke in Acts 19 that was the scene of a tremendous riot has been unearthed. I have stood in that theater where thousands of angry Ephesians wanted to kill Paul's associates for ruining their idol-making business.

Space does not permit me to describe a multitude of other archaeological confirmations of biblical names, events, and locations. While it is true that both the size and the scope of such discoveries cannot prove the Bible is true, it is important to note that there has never been any discovery that has *disproved* any name, event, or location in the Bible.

Dr. Nelson Glueck, a respected authority on Israeli archaeology, writes, "No archeological discovery has ever controverted a Biblical reference. Scores of archeological findings have been made which confirm in clear outline or in exact detail historical statements in the Bible. And, by the same token, proper evaluation of Biblical descriptions has often led to amazing discoveries."[21]

"BUT WHAT ABOUT . . ."

In spite of the overwhelming evidence for the trustworthiness of the Bible, many have legitimate questions about the Bible they hold in their hands. Here are three of the most common objections to the authenticity of the Bible.

Objection #1: "Scribes Made Errors in Copying Texts throughout the Centuries"

Even if you accept that the original manuscripts of the Bible were without error, isn't it logical to assume that those who copied the Scriptures throughout the centuries made errors either intentionally or unintentionally, resulting in a text that is probably far removed than what was originally written? Such a concern is easily dismissed when one looks at the number of manuscripts that exist and the minor variations between manuscripts that have occurred.

Most ancient literary works have very few manuscripts to support their authenticity. There are only seven for Plato, eight for Herodotus, ten for Caesar's *Gallic Wars*, and twenty for the historian Tacitus. Yet there are over ten thousand manuscripts for the Old Testament. The most amazing manuscript discovery occurred in 1947 at Qumran near the Dead Sea.

A young Bedouin herdsman found some clay jars hidden in a cave that contained scrolls of the Old Testament hidden by a commune of monastic farmers. These "Dead Sea Scrolls" are dated around 100 BC and contain a complete copy of Isaiah, along with fragments of almost every book of the Old Testament. What caused many to hail this discovery as the greatest archaeological find of the twentieth century is that it predates the oldest manuscripts of the Old Testament by nearly one thousand years. Prior to the finding of these scrolls at the Dead Sea, the earliest complete copy of the Old Testament was the Masoretic Text, which was dated around AD 900.

One of the greatest values of the Dead Sea Scrolls is that they allow scholars to compare the accuracy of manuscript transmission over a thousand-year period of time. You would think that the constant process of copying the same material over a millennium by a variety of people would result in numerous errors. Instead, the Dead Sea Scrolls reveal how accurately the text was copied over time. For example, there was a word-for-word identity in 95 percent of the text. Of the 166 words in Isaiah 53, there were only seventeen letters in question, and ten of those were simply due to spelling, four letters related to minor issues like conjunctions, and the three remaining letters in question spelled the word "light," which is found in verse 11. This one questionable word does not alter in any significant way the meaning of the text. In other words, after one thousand years of copying 166 words, only one word is in question—and it is a word that is insignificant to the meaning of the text.

The manuscript support for the New Testament is even more overwhelming. Without doubt, the books of the New Testament were the most frequently copied of any books of antiquity. Today we have nearly twenty-five thousand copies of portions of the New Testament. Contrast that to Homer's *Iliad*, which is next in terms of the number of available manuscripts. Only 643 copies of it are in existence. There is more—and earlier—manuscript support for the Jesus Christ found in the Gospels than for any other figure in the ancient world, including Julius Caesar and Alexander the Great.

The amount of time between the writing of the original books of the New Testament and the earliest, existing manuscript copies is only several hundred years. Although that sounds like a long time, it isn't when compared to other works of literature. The oldest manuscripts of most classical Greek authors are dated more than one thousand years after the authors' deaths (the plays of Sophocles are based on manuscripts that are dated fourteen hundred years after the poet's death). Yet we possess many partial manuscripts of the New Testament that are only one hundred years removed from the originals.

Most importantly, these manuscripts reveal how accurately the New Testament has been transmitted throughout the centuries. The Greek New Testament contains about twenty thousand lines of text. Only about forty lines are in question because of variations among the manuscripts (that amounts to one page in the two-hundred-page Greek New Testament).

Greek scholars like the late A. T. Robertson claim that the variations only account for "a thousandth part of the entire text," meaning that the New Testament text we have today is 99.9 percent pure.[22] It is important to note that those few variations concern minor details such as whether or not an article goes before a noun. As Arthur Patzia notes, "No significant doctrine of the New Testament hinges on a variant."[23]

Objection #2: "The Selection of the Books in Our Bible Was Arbitrary"

A central theme of Dan Brown's best-selling novel *The Da Vinci Code* is that the compilation of books that comprise the Bible we have today is the result of a power grab by the Roman emperor Constantine in the fourth century. According to Brown, prior to the fourth century the early church didn't claim that Jesus Christ was divine. The "true" accounts of Christ's life (known as the Gnostic Gospels, which portrayed Jesus as merely human) were burned by Constantine, who then invented a new Bible that presented Christ as the divine Son of God. One of Dan Brown's main characters, Sir Leigh Teabing, says, "The Bible is a product of man, my dear. Not of God. . . . History has never had a definitive version of the book. . . . The Bible, as we know it today, was collated by the pagan Roman emperor Constantine the Great."[24]

How can we know that the Bible we have today is, in fact, the right Bible? What about those other books that were omitted from our Bible—do they have important information we need to know that would change our beliefs? And why is there a difference between the Catholic Bible and the Protestant Bible? All of these questions deal with the canon of Scripture. The word *canon* means "measuring rod" and refers to the books in the Bible that were deemed to "measure up to" the standards required for a book to be considered as God's Word.

First, let's look at the thirty-nine books that make up the Old Testament we have today. With just a few exceptions, all of the books of the Old Testament were immediately recognized as the Word of God after they were written. Norman Geisler explains,

> When Moses wrote the first five books of the Bible, they were taken immediately and put in the most holy place (Dt. 31:24-26). The book of Joshua, his successor, was added to the collection upon his death (Jos. 24:26). Likewise the books of Samuel (1 Sm. 10:25) and the prophets were added after they wrote them (Zech. 7:12). Daniel had a collection of Moses' books and the prophetic writings up to Daniel's time, including the book of his contemporary, Jeremiah. (Dan. 9:2)[25]

It is worth noting that there were other books of Jewish religious literature that were quoted in the Old Testament but were not included, such as the book of Jashar and the book of Wars.

Many people erroneously believe that the Old Testament canon was still fluid during the time of Christ and was not finalized until the Council of Jamnia met in AD 90. However, the truth is that the Council of Jamnia only ratified the books of the Old Testament that the Jews had already recognized hundreds of years earlier. Many scholars believe that the Old Testament canon was closed as early as 400 BC and certainly no later than 250 BC to 150 BC. How do we know that? The

Greek translation of the Old Testament (known as the Septuagint) was translated between 250 BC and 150 BC and contains all of the books that are in our Old Testament today.

However, it should be noted that later versions of Septuagint contain additional books, some of which are part of a collection known as the Apocrypha (meaning "hidden" or "doubtful") and are included in the Catholic Bible. These books were written between 250 BC and 100 BC, contain historical errors, and have not been recognized by Jews as part of the Old Testament. Significantly, none of these books claims to contain the Word of God as do other books in the Old Testament.

Neither Jesus nor the apostles ever quoted from any books in the Apocrypha. Jerome, the Roman Catholic scholar who translated the Latin Vulgate Bible, rejected these books. The Roman Catholic Church did not officially ratify these books until sixteen hundred years after they were written! Although these books contain some interesting historical information, they have never been recognized, even by the Roman Catholic Church, to be equal in authority with the Old Testament.

There are equally compelling reasons to believe that the twenty-seven books contained in our New Testament are the correct books. First, virtually every one of these books was written either by an apostle (like Peter or Paul) or was written under the supervision of an apostle (Mark's gospel was most likely written under Peter's supervision).

Furthermore, the majority of all the New Testament books were written between AD 45 and AD 100. That means the Gospels were penned only a few years after Christ's death and resurrection, greatly minimizing the corruption of the text by the addition of spurious stories. As noted earlier, Peter recognized Paul's letters as scripture (2 Peter 3:15–16), meaning he believed they possessed the same authority as the Old Testament. Paul affirmed Luke's gospel as scripture in 1 Timothy 5:18, and Jude quoted from Peter in Jude 17–18.

The Council of Hippo officially ratified the twenty-seven books in our New Testament in AD 393, but the majority of those books were received and recognized by the early church hundreds of years earlier. Significantly, there has been no attempt to add to or delete from the canon of the New Testament since its ratification at the end of the fourth century.

What about the Gnostic Gospels that Dan Brown's *The Da Vinci Code* describes? Are there more reliable accounts of Jesus' life that were "outlawed, gathered up, and burned" because they presented Jesus as merely a man? It is true that there are five or six writings that comprise the Gnostic Bible. However, these books were not included in the canon of the New Testament for very sound reasons. First, none was written by the apostles, who were eyewitnesses to Jesus' life (even though some bear the names of apostles). Second, these books were written between one hundred and two hundred years after the time of Christ, making them far less reliable than the Gospels in the New Testament, which were written within decades of Jesus' life on earth.

Finally, these Gnostic Gospels were rejected by church leaders because they denied the humanity of Jesus Christ, not because they emphasized His humanity. The Gnostics embraced a dualistic philosophy that labeled anything material as evil. Therefore, the Gnostics denied Jesus' humanity and taught He was only a divine Spirit. While the early church leaders were certainly aware of the Gnostic Gospels, they never argued for or even considered their inclusion in the canon of the New Testament.

Objection #3: "The Bible Contains Too Many Errors and Contradictions to Be Trustworthy"

Perhaps you have heard that the Bible contains numerous errors and contradictions. But is that really true? Some of the so-called errors in the Bible can be attributed to accepted literary devices such as the language of appearance. For example, critics of the Bible cite Isaiah 11:12

as an example of a mistake in the Bible: "And [He] will gather the dispersed of Judah from the four corners of the earth."

Was Isaiah claiming the earth is flat by referring to the "four corners of the earth"? Of course not! He was no more mistaken than is the meteorologist on television who reports the time for "sunrise" and "sunset." The weatherman is not claiming that the sun actually rises and sets but, like Isaiah, is simply using the language of appearance.

A few of the alleged errors in the Bible can be attributed to copyists' errors. Remember, when we say that the Bible is without error we are speaking about the original manuscripts, not the numerous copies that emanated from them down through the centuries. As we saw in the last section, the number of copyists' errors are remarkably few, but some do exist and are easy to identify.

For example, the Masoretic text of 2 Chronicles 22:2 says that Ahaziah was forty-two, yet 2 Kings 8:26 says that Ahaziah was twenty-two. Had Ahaziah been forty-two, he would have been older than his father! Obviously, the scribe made an error. Another example is 2 Chronicles 9:25, which claims that Solomon had four thousand horse stalls while 1 Kings 4:26 says it was forty thousand stalls. The forty-thousand number is probably a copyist's mistake since Solomon only had twelve thousand horsemen.

I realize that the scribe-made-error explanation could be a catch-all rationale for every discrepancy in the Bible. However, as noted previously, these kinds of mistakes are very rare. Also, the context and parallel passages make it relatively easy to identify the errant passage. Most importantly, none of these minor errors affects any major doctrine of the Bible.

Some of the often-cited mistakes in the Bible are not mistakes at all when you examine the original languages. For example, in Matthew 13:32 Jesus referred to the mustard seed as the "least of all seeds," as it is translated in the King James Version. Did Jesus make a mistake since we know there are seeds smaller than the mustard seed? The word translated "least" is not a superlative but a comparative word in the Greek language, and it is correctly rendered as "smaller" in the New American Standard Bible. In other words, Jesus was simply placing the mustard seed in a category of small seeds, not claiming that it was the absolute smallest of any seed in the earth.

Similarly, many of the claimed contradictions in the Bible are not contradictions at all when carefully studied. For example, as we have seen, in 1 Corinthians 10:8 Paul describes a God-sent plague in the Old Testament that killed twenty-three thousand Israelites in a single day. Yet, the original account in Numbers 25:9 claims that twenty-four thousand died. Who is correct: Paul or Moses? Both are telling the truth. Paul says that twenty-three thousand Israelites "fell in one day," while Moses claims that the total number of victims was twenty-four thousand. Most likely, not everyone who contracted the plague died within a twenty-four hour period of time. On a single day twenty-three thousand died, while the total casualty list was twenty-four thousand.

Other alleged contradictions are the result of failing to distinguish between exact quotations and paraphrases. For example, some people are disturbed by the different accounts of Jesus' words in the Gospels. Why is Luke's account of the Sermon on the Mount (Luke 6) so much shorter than Matthew's account (Matthew 5–7)? It could be that Jesus preached this message in two different locations at two different times. Or Luke could have simply been summarizing Jesus' message.

Although the English language expresses exactness of quotations with quotation marks, there are no quotation marks in the Greek language that would inherently claim word-for-word precision. The gospel writers, guided and protected from error by the Holy Spirit, could have paraphrased Jesus' words and still accurately conveyed His message. For example, if I were to say in a sermon, "No one under twenty-one should ever marry" and a person in the audience was to later say to a friend, "The pastor said today that eighteen-year-olds should not marry," would he be accurately representing what I said? Yes, even though that person was not quoting me word-for-word, he would be communicating the essence of my message. The definition of *inerrancy* that we have established allows for free quotation and paraphrases.

Some of the alleged contradictions in the Bible are the result of complementary accounts of the same event. For example, imagine I were describing a wreck on the highway to a friend and said, "Three ambulances surrounded the demolished cars." Yet, suppose someone else said to my friend, "I drove by the wreck and saw three ambulances and two fire trucks at the scene of the accident." Was my account of the accident scene erroneous because I omitted seeing the fire trucks? Not at all. Perhaps the fire trucks came after I passed by the scene. Or maybe I focused solely on the ambulances because they signaled to me that people had been seriously injured.

Similarly, the Bible—especially the Gospels—sometimes provide differing accounts of the same story. For example, Matthew records that there was one angel at Jesus' tomb (Matthew 28:1–2), and John says there were two angels there (John 20:12). Are these contradictory accounts? Only if Matthew had claimed there was *only* one angel present at the tomb. Possibly Matthew decided to focus on the one angel who spoke, while John was more interested in the total number of angels Mary witnessed when she arrived at the tomb.

Divergent accounts of the same event (as long as they are not blatantly contradictory) actually argue for rather than against the credibility of the writers. For example, over the last few weeks a magazine writer has been working on a story about me and my ministry. He has interviewed numerous friends and associates and often asked them to recount a story he has heard about me from another source. He told me that if the accounts are word-for-word identical to one another he is suspicious that the interviewees have colluded with one another (or me) to make sure we are pushing the same story rather than telling the truth. If an event actually occurred, it is only natural that different witnesses of that event would offer different (but not contradictory) accounts of that event.

A LETTER YOU CAN TRUST

In his book *The Ten(Der) Commandments* Ron Mehl says he has talked to a number of friends who have received letters and cards from their mothers through the years. But that number of communiqués drops dramatically when it comes to fathers. If someone receives a letter from his father the immediate reaction is "Who died?" or "This is a major event. Something big must have happened." Mehl writes, "Something big has happened. Your Father took time to write, and it was such an important letter that He literally wrote it with His own hand. . . . He wanted to make sure that in those times when we long for counsel about which way to turn, we'd know just what to do."[26]

God took the initiative in communicating His message to you for one reason: He loves you. And because God is all-powerful you can rest assured that He has both the ability and the motivation to make sure that His message has been communicated to you without error. That is the best reason for knowing that the Bible is true.

CHAPTER THREE

HOW CAN I KNOW CHRISTIANITY IS THE RIGHT RELIGION?

In the fall of 2011, I traveled to Washington D.C. to introduce presidential candidate governor Rick Perry at the Values Voters Summit. After Governor Perry's speech, I left the ballroom and was swarmed by dozens of television and print reporters who were shouting a variety of questions at me. One reporter asked me if I believed Mormons were Christians (a relevant question since two of the announced Republican presidential candidates were Mormons). I replied, "Mormons are good, moral people. But Mormonism is not Christianity; it is a cult."

My statement was the shot heard 'round the world. Within minutes my words became the "Breaking News" on CNN for the next seven hours. My cell phone rang continuously with requests for interviews from cable news networks, the *Washington Post*, the *New York Times*, and *Newsweek*. During the following week I was interviewed by everyone from Chris Matthews to Bill Maher. One evening a few weeks later I was driving home listening to one of the Republican presidential debates and nearly drove off the freeway when I heard governor Mitt Romney demand that Governor Perry "denounce Pastor Jeffress" for my pronouncement about the Mormon faith. Then I knew I had pierced the cultural consciousness when I was referred to in a skit on *Saturday Night Live*.

The negative newspaper and magazine editorials from the secular press were predictable. The flood of obscene phone calls and e-mails from unbelievers was expected. But what genuinely surprised me was the vitriolic reaction from many professing Christians who could not fathom someone declaring that a popular religious belief system like Mormonism would not lead someone to heaven. Some thought my use of the term *cult* was over-the-top. But my attempt to clarify my remarks by differentiating between "theological cult" (a group with a human founder and a separate religious book apart from the Bible) versus a "sociological cult" (think Branch Davidians) did not satisfy my critics. What bothered people was the fact that I judged any other religious system to be an invalid path leading to eternal life. One woman wrote:

> I am a Christian from Wisconsin. I saw your interview on CNN today. I was saddened, angered and appalled by your comments. It's interesting that you are a "pastor" considering your sentiments go against the very tenets and teachings of the Bible, one of which is "thou shalt not judge." Your beliefs are bigoted and border on racist. Fortunately, your sentiment is a fading one, a view that is reflective of an America that was filled with hate, discrimination and egregious acts that were all justified in the name of the Bible! Luckily, America has grown full of acceptance, forgiveness and charity, the tenets of what Jesus spoke to everyone. Lastly, even though I am embarrassed as a Christian by your remarks, I will pray that other non-Christians recognize you for what you really are. I am going to sic God after you and let Him fix your hate-filled heart!

I wholeheartedly agree with this woman on one point: the sentiment that there is only one correct way to God is "a fading one." According to a poll from the Barna Group in 2011, 40 percent of Americans surveyed agreed with the statement, "All people are eventually saved or accepted by God, no matter what they do, because he loves all people he has created." Twenty-six percent of those identifying themselves as born-again Christians agreed with the statement, "It doesn't matter what religious faith you follow because they all teach the same lessons."[1] A 2008 poll of thirty-five thousand Americans revealed that "57 percent of evangelical church attenders said they believe that many religions can lead to eternal life."[2] Regardless of which poll you believe, it is obvious that a significant number of Christians do not accept the proposition that there is only one "right" religion.

WHICH GOD?

The implications of rejecting the notion that faith in the Jesus Christ of the Bible for the forgiveness of sins offers the only hope for eternal life are obvious. On a personal level, how do I know which god I should be worshipping and what that god requires of me? When I pray, am I addressing Allah of Islam, Jehovah God of the Bible, or one of the many gods in Hinduism? And exactly which path do I follow in order to experience eternal life: the practice of the four yogas of Hinduism, the Noble Eightfold Path of Buddhism, the Mosaic code of Judaism, or the laws of Allah found in the Qur'an? If you say that it doesn't really matter which path you take, then are you saying that Christianity, Islam, Buddhism, and Mormonism are all wrong belief systems since they claim an exclusive way to eternal life? (Of the world's major religions, only Hinduism teaches that all religions lead to God.)

The consequences of embracing inclusivism (the belief that all religions lead to God) extend to our relationships with other people. Why risk offending someone of a different faith by sharing your beliefs about Jesus Christ if that person is headed toward the same heaven as you? Why give your hard-earned money to support mission efforts around the world if all religions are equally valid?

Ultimately, inclusivism affects your view of Jesus Christ. The Christian who believes that all people will be in heaven regardless of their religious faith must reject some of Jesus' clearest teachings about the exclusive nature of His message.

- Was Jesus wrong when He spoke of a narrow way that leads to eternal life and a broad way that leads to eternal destruction? (Matthew 7:13–14)
- Was Jesus being intolerant by declaring that no person could come to God except through Him? (John 14:6)
- Was Jesus demonstrating hatred toward others when He taught regularly about the reality of a hell that will be populated with people who had rejected His message? (John 3:18)

If Jesus was in error about these key issues, how can we trust anything He said?

In his book *Is God a Christian?* R. Kirby Godsey, former president of Mercer University and a self-identified Baptist, argues against the idea that there is only one way to God. In an interview about the book, Godsey claimed:

Those of us who have grown up in the Christian tradition think it's rather obvious that God belongs to our tradition. We assume God is one of us. But it's just as apparent to people who grew up in different religions that God's Word and God's ways are not the exclusive property of the Christian tradition. There are people of genuine piety and profound religious conviction who have come to that piety through other avenues. . . . God is not a Christian. God is not a Jew. God is not a Hindu. God is above all our perceptions and all our expressions of God. . . . This in no way diminishes my own Christian commitment. We should never assume that the validity of the Christian tradition is dependent on the invalidity of every other tradition.[3]

Yet the belief that there are multiple avenues to God *should* diminish—and ultimately extinguish—any thinking person's "Christian commitment" because it destroys the credibility of the Founder of the Christian faith, Jesus Christ.

ERRONEOUS BELIEFS ABOUT EXCLUSIVISM

Why do so many people reject exclusivism—the belief that faith in Jesus Christ is the only means by which a person can experience a relationship with God? Many have erroneous ideas about exclusivism.

Error #1: Exclusivism Is Intolerant

In our society tolerance is celebrated as the highest of all virtues. Being accused of intolerance is tantamount to being labeled as a drug dealer or child molester. Most people equate tolerance with the rejection of all moral and spiritual absolutes. To be tolerant of homosexuals means that you are unwilling to label homosexuality as a sin. To be tolerant of Hindus means that you accept Hinduism as an equally valid avenue to God as Christianity.

However, if you claim that faith in Jesus Christ is the exclusive means of salvation, you are demonstrating intolerance toward other people, and intolerance leads toward hatred and ultimately to the oppression of others. R. Kirby Godsey makes the leap from exclusivism to violence:

> I don't think that all fundamentalists are bad people. But there's not a dime's worth of difference between Christian, Jewish, Muslim or Hindu fundamentalists. They're all cut from the same cloth. Fundamentalist exclusivity, where God is identified with the Christian order, and therefore everything that challenges that social order is a challenge to God and should be a challenge to all Christians and humanity, seems to lead to the kind of terrible human

tragedy we witnessed in Norway [a reference to a shooting spree by a man who claimed to be defending Christianity].[4]

However, as I point out in my book *Twilight's Last Gleaming*, there is a vast difference between what I term "pseudo-tolerance" that is in vogue today and the historic understanding of what I call "true tolerance."[5] *Tolerance* means "to allow or to permit, to recognize and respect others' beliefs and practices without sharing them, to bear or put up with someone or something not necessarily liked."[6]

To be tolerant of another person does not require surrendering my convictions that certain behaviors and beliefs are wrong. I can respect a homosexual without accepting homosexuality as a viable lifestyle choice. I can recognize and respect a Muslim and still retain my belief that Christianity offers the only the pathway to God. In fact, inherent in the definition of *tolerance* is a fundamental disagreement with the person you are tolerating.

There is no great virtue in demonstrating respect for someone with whom you agree or who engage in a behavior about which you have no strong conviction. I have no problem tolerating people who are evangelical Christians (a perspective I share) or who play croquet (a sport for which I have no strong feelings). Genuine tolerance requires respect for those behavior and beliefs about which you *disagree*.

This very important distinction is lost on many Americans, in part because of our Constitution's guarantee of freedom of religious expression. A man who identified himself as a member of a conservative Christian denomination sent me an angry letter recently over my insistence that Christianity offers the only legitimate path to God:

I thought Christians were tolerant of other religions, that they believe the United States was established so *all* people could worship according to their desires. . . . Shame, shame, on you for talking about things you have no knowledge of—you are a son of the devil if you are not tolerant of *all* religions.

Apparently, this person has no tolerance for those he considers to be intolerant! But beyond obvious hypocrisy of his pronouncement, his comments reflect the confusion between tolerance and relativism. Our country grants everyone the right to worship (or not to worship) as he chooses, just as God grants us the freedom to choose whom we will worship.

But granting that right does not necessitate embracing relativism—the idea that all belief systems are equally valid. When Joshua challenged the Israelites to "choose for yourselves today whom you will serve" (Joshua 24:15), he was not suggesting that Jehovah God or the pagan deity Baal were equally valid options! Joshua was simply recognizing every individual's God-given right and responsibility to make his own choice about which religious belief system to embrace. Tolerance means "I respect your right to be wrong."

Error #2: Exclusivism Is Unnecessary

Another objection to Christianity's claim of exclusivity is that it is unnecessary, given the alleged similarities of all religions. According to the famous playwright George Bernard Shaw, "There is only one religion, though there are hundreds of versions of it."[6] Many people have bought into the idea that no one religion can claim to possess all the truth about God. Instead, different religions express various realities about the same God. The parable of the three blind men and the elephant is often used to illustrate that claim.

Imagine that three blind men are each touching an elephant in different places. The first blind man touches the elephant's trunk and says, "I believe an elephant is like a snake." The second blind man, while touching the elephant's leg, says, "You're wrong. An elephant is like a great trunk of a tree." The third blind man, touching the side of the massive animal, says, "You both are wrong. An elephant is like a brick wall." Each of the men thinks he is right and the others are wrong. But, in fact, they are all describing different parts of the same elephant. So it is with God, we are told. Every religion is describing different truths about the same deity, but each religion is only able to grasp a part of the total picture.

However, there are two obvious problems with this analogy. First, the story of the blind men assumes the men were indeed touching an elephant. How do we know the first man was touching an elephant instead of an oak tree? The story assumes there was an elephant that had very defined characteristics—it was a massive creature rather than a slithering reptile, it had large legs, and a trunk. In other words, there were objective realities about this creature that the men were attempting to define according to their finite understanding. The elephant was not the sum of these three men's descriptions of it but possessed definitive attributes apart from these men's speculations.

The second problem with this analogy is that it does not allow for contradictory claims about the nature of the elephant. Notice that all three men were touching different parts of the elephant and, thus, giving different descriptions of what the elephant was like. But suppose all three were touching the same part of the elephant: the leg. One man says, "The elephant is a strong tree." Another man says, "No, the elephant feels like a pliable snowball that I can crush with my hands." And the third man, suffering from leprosy and, therefore unable to feel anything, says, "I can't feel anything at all. The elephant must not exist." Each of these three men is making a claim that contradicts the other two, and therefore, only one of the three men can be correct. Either the elephant's leg is like a sturdy tree, a snowball, or it doesn't exist.

Author Dinesh D'Souza claims that there are only two groups of people that allege that all religions are the same: atheists and well-meaning but uninformed religious people.[7] To those who do not believe in any God, all religions are simply variations of the same myths. Atheist Richard Dawkins writes in his book A *Devil's Chaplain*: "When it comes to Baal and the Golden Calf, Thor, and Wotan, Poseidon and Apollo, Mithras and Ammon Ra" modern theists are "actually atheists. . . . Some of us just go one god further."[8]

The only other group of people who believe that all religions make the same truth claims are those who are ignorant of the teachings of the major world religions. For example, there is a vast difference among various religions about the most basic concept regarding God. Islam, Judaism, and Christianity insist there is only one God. Hinduism allows for millions of deities. Buddhism, on the other hand, does not teach the existence of a personal God, and those Buddhists who do believe in God tend to view God as nothing more than the sum total of creation.

Various religions also are in disagreement about the basic problem confronting humanity. Hindus diagnose man's challenge as "samsara" —the endless cycle of birth, death, and reincarnation. Only by understanding one's relationship to Brahman can this cycle be broken. Islam teaches man's basic problem is a failure to keep the laws of Allah as revealed in the Qur'an. Only by accumulating enough good works to off-set our evil deeds, with a sprinkling of Allah's grace, can one hope to be welcomed into heaven. The Qur'an states, "Then those whose balance [of good deeds] is heavy, they will be successful. But those whose balance is light, will be those who have lost their souls; in hell will they abide" (Qur'an 23:102–103).

Christianity declares that mankind's chief problem is a failure to keep a different set of laws issued by a different deity. However, unlike Islam, Christianity does not allow a person to work himself back into that deity's favor. Instead, Christianity teaches that one must repent of his sins and place his faith in Jesus Christ for salvation.

Another vast difference exists between various religions regarding what happens to a person when he dies. Hindus believe that humans are trapped in an endless cycle of life, death, and rebirth that starts again when we die. Islam teaches that we die once and then are judged by Allah. Mormons believe that those who die and have not repented of their sins are dispatched to a temporary hell where they are given instruction and another opportunity to repent. Christians have historically believed that once a person dies, all opportunities for repentance are over and a person's eternal fate is sealed forever.

Interestingly, the founders or leading advocates for some of the world's major religions proudly trumpeted how their faith was different rather than similar to other religious belief systems. For example, the Buddha was a dissatisfied follower of Hinduism who rejected the idea that man's basic problem was a failure to recognize himself as a divine being, thus sentencing himself to an endless cycle of birth, death, and rebirth. Instead, the Buddha theorized that man's basic flaw was an insatiable desire for pleasure, status, and the other necessities of life. Only by following the Noble Eightfold Path could one find true satisfaction in life and enter into that restful state of nirvana.

Both Abraham, the father of the Israelites, and the lawgiver Moses rejected the polytheistic beliefs popular in their day and taught that there was only one true God. Muhammad, the founder of Islam, also turned away from belief in multiple deities and taught that Allah was the only true God. Peter, the leader of Jesus' apostles, declared that all other paths to God other than Jesus Christ were dead-end roads: "And there is salvation in no one else; for there is no other name under heaven that has been given among men, by which we must be saved" (Acts 4:12).

Both the existence of various religions and the intense strife that has existed between the followers of those religions is due to the differences, not the similarities, between those contrasting belief systems. As Christian apologist Ravi Zacharias writes, "Every religion at its core is exclusive."[9]

Error #3: Exclusivism Is Troubling

I believe that the core reason that all non-Christians and many Christians reject the exclusive truth claims of Christianity is the obvious and disturbing conclusion that most people have embraced the wrong religion. And if Christianity is true, then the majority of people in the world today—along with the majority of people who have ever lived—are destined to an eternity in hell. After all, only 25 percent of the 7 billion people in the world today even claim to be Christians, meaning that nearly 5 billion people are sincerely following a system of belief (or unbelief) that will result in their eternal damnation. How can so many sincere people be so wrong?

Author Bruce Nicholls believes there are two basic attributes of human beings that answer this question. First, human beings by nature are "insatiably religious." He notes that for twenty-five hundred years millions of sincere Hindus have prayed daily the sacred Upanishadic prayer: "From delusion lead me to truth. From darkness lead me to light. From death lead me to immortality."[10] Our natural inclination for reaching out to someone or something greater than ourselves is the result of being created in God's image. As Solomon observed, God has "set eternity in their heart" (Ecclesiastes 3:11). Because man is more than a collection of dust and chemicals, it is only natural that the spirit God has placed in him yearns to connect with that which is spiritual.

But why does man's innate spirituality lead the majority of people to the wrong God? Nicholls explains that in addition to being insatiably religious, man is also "incurably rebellious."[11]

One of the residual effects of the sin virus we have all inherited as a result of the Fall is the inborn propensity to reject the knowledge of the true God (along with His commands) and replace it with a god more of our own liking. In Romans 1 the apostle Paul explains the threefold process by which the majority of humans have received knowledge of the true God through creation, have rejected that revelation, and have replaced that knowledge of the true God with a god of their own making:

> For since the creation of the world His invisible attributes, His eternal power and divine nature, have been clearly seen, being understood through what has been made, so that they are without excuse. . . . Professing to be wise, they became fools, and exchanged the glory of the incorruptible God for an image in the form of corruptible man and of birds and four-footed animals and crawling creatures. (Romans 1:20, 22–23)

Why don't the majority of people in the world ever find the true God? The same reason a bank robber never seems to be able to find a policeman! The vast majority of people are attempting to hide from the true God (and His demands) just as Adam and Eve hid from their Creator in the garden.

Yet there is that ever-present desire—admittedly stronger in some than in others—to worship that which is greater than themselves. The rejection and replacement of the knowledge of the true God with another god (whether it be an imaginary deity, a self-serving philosophy, or an all-consuming pursuit) is man's way to satisfy his religious drive that has been corrupted by sin. However, if Christianity does offer the only pathway to eternal life, then the implication for the majority of mankind is truly troubling.

WHAT MAKES CHRISTIANITY UNIQUE?

Obviously, any religion or philosophy can claim exclusivity. How can we know that Christianity is indeed the right religion?

The Uniqueness of Jesus Christ

Few historians doubt that Jesus actually existed. Even the deist Thomas Paine, who believed the Bible was filled with errors and inconsistences, accepted the historicity of Jesus. However, Paine embraced the view of Jesus that the majority of non-Christians have today:

> He [Jesus Christ] was a virtuous and an amiable man. The morality that he preached and practiced was of the most benevolent kind; and though similar systems of morality had been preached by Confucius, and by some of the Greek philosophers, many years before; by the Quakers since; and by many good men in all ages, it has not been exceeded by any.[12]

But the problem with believing that Jesus was only a great moral teacher like others who preceded and succeeded Him is that He claimed to be more—much more—than that. In fact, no other philosopher or religious leader before or since Jesus has ever made the claims that Jesus made. For example . . .

Jesus claimed to be God. Although many religious leaders and philosophers have attempted to point people toward God, none of them has ever claimed to be God. For example, the prophet Muhammad, the founder of Islam, said, "Surely I am no more than a human apostle."[13] Muhammad's confession is not unique. Moses, Confucius, the Buddha, Joseph Smith, and Lao Tse never portrayed themselves to be anything more than sinful men.[14]

However, Jesus claimed to be equal to God Himself. In John 10:30 Jesus declared, "I and the Father are one." When Philip begged Jesus to "show us the Father, and it is enough for us" (John 14:8), Jesus responded to his request by saying, "Have I been so long with you, and yet you have not come to know Me, Philip? He who has seen me has seen the Father; how can you say, 'Show us the Father'?" (John 14:9).

Eighty-two times in the Gospels Jesus refers to Himself as "the Son of Man." Many readers wrongly assume that this title refers to the humanity of Christ. However, those Jews who were listening to Jesus knew exactly what He was saying by using that phrase to describe

Himself. The Old Testament prophet Daniel used the term "Son of Man" to refer to the Messiah who would one day rule over all of the earth:

> I kept looking in the night visions, and behold, with the clouds of heaven One like a Son of Man was coming, and He came up to the Ancient of Days and was presented before Him. And to Him was given dominion, glory and a kingdom, that all the peoples, nations and men of every language might serve Him. His dominion is an everlasting dominion which will not pass away; and his kingdom is one which will not be destroyed. (Daniel 7:13–14)

During one of the trials prior to Jesus' crucifixion, the Jewish high priest Caiaphas asked Jesus point-blank: "Are You the Christ, the Son of the Blessed One?" (Mark 14:61). Jesus answered, "I am" and then He added the quote from Daniel 7:13: "and you shall see THE SON OF MAN SITTING AT THE RIGHT HAND OF POWER AND COMING WITH THE CLOUDS OF HEAVEN" (Mark 16:62).

Caiaphas and the members of the Sanhedrin (the ruling council of the Jews) understood perfectly that Jesus was declaring Himself to be the long-awaited Son of God, whom the Jews understood to be God Himself. If there is any doubt as to what Jesus was claiming for Himself, notice Caiaphas' response to Jesus' words:

> Tearing his clothes, the high priest said, "What further need do we have of witnesses? You have heard the blasphemy; how does it seem to you?" And they all condemned Him to be deserving of death. (Mark 14:63–64)

One more example. In John 8 the Jewish religious leaders engaged Jesus in a discussion about His relationship with Abraham, the revered patriarch of Judaism. Jesus flabbergasted His audience by declaring,

"Your father Abraham rejoiced to see My day, and he saw it and was glad." . . . "Truly, truly I say to you, before Abraham was born, I am" (John 8:56, 58). Jesus was claiming to have lived before Abraham, who had been dead for nearly two thousand years!

If Jesus had only been referring to His eternal existence, He would have said, "Before Abraham was born, I was." However, the term "I am" had great significance to the religious leaders. They knew the words "I AM" represented the most holy name for God (Yahweh) in the Old Testament. It was the name God used for Himself when speaking to Moses at the burning bush (Exodus 3:14). By using the words "I am" Jesus was not just claiming to be a prophet of God or some lesser version of God, He was declaring that He was God Himself. The Jewish leaders were so enraged by what they perceived to be Jesus' blasphemous statement that they "picked up stones to throw at Him" (John 8:59).

Jesus claimed to forgive sins. No other religious leader or philosopher ever claimed the ability to forgive people of their sins and grant them eternal life. For example, the Buddha said, ". . . in reality there are no living beings to whom the Lord Buddha can bring salvation."[15] Yet Jesus believed that He had the authority to forgive people of their sins.

For example, Mark 2 records a group of disciples bringing a paralytic man to Jesus. "And Jesus seeing their faith said to the paralytic, Son, your sins are forgiven" (Mark 2:5). The religious leaders, infuriated by Jesus' declaration, asked, "Why does this man speak that way? He is blaspheming; who can forgive sins but God alone?" (v. 7). Jesus answered their question with a visual demonstration of His authority:

"But so that you may know that the Son of Man has authority on earth to forgive sins"—He said to the paralytic, "I say to you, get up, pick up your pallet and go home." And he got up and immediately picked up the pallet and went out in the sight of everyone, so that they were all amazed and were glorifying God, saying, "We have never seen anything like this." (vv. 10–12)

Jesus consistently taught that His primary purpose in leaving heaven and coming into the world was not just to point people to the path of forgiveness from God but through His death to be the means by which people can be forgiven by God:

- "For the Son of Man has come to seek and to save that which was lost" (Luke 19:10).
- "Just as the Son of Man did not come to be served, but to serve, and to give His life as a ransom for many" (Matthew 20:28).
- "As Moses lifted up the serpent in the wilderness, even so must the Son of Man be lifted up; that whoever believes will in Him have eternal life. For God so loved the world, that He gave His only begotten Son, that whoever believes in Him shall not perish, but have eternal life" (John 3:14–16).
- "I am the resurrection and the life; he who believes in Me will live even if he dies" (John 11:25).

Jesus claimed to conquer death. Jesus repeatedly prophesied that He would be killed by His enemies and then rise from the dead three days later:

From that time Jesus began to show His disciples that He must go to Jerusalem, and suffer many things from the elders and chief priests and scribes, and be killed, and be raised up on the third day. (Matthew 16:21)

And Jesus said to them, "You will all fall away, because it is written, 'I WILL STRIKE DOWN THE SHEPHERD, AND THE SHEEP SHALL BE SCATTERED.' But after I have been raised, I will go ahead of you to Galilee." (Mark 14:27–28)

Furthermore, Jesus taught that His resurrection from the dead would be the signal proof that He was the Son of God:

Then some of the scribes and Pharisees said to Him, "Teacher, we want to see a sign from you." But He answered and said to them, "An evil and adulterous generation craves for a sign; and yet no sign will be given to it but the sign of Jonah the prophet; for just as JONAH WAS THREE DAYS AND THREE NIGHTS IN THE BELLY OF THE SEA MONSTER, so will the Son of Man be three days and three nights in the heart of the earth." (Matthew 12:38–40)

In other words, just as Jonah remained in the belly of the great fish *only* three days and nights, Jesus was predicting that His stay in the grave would be only temporary. If you think that it is too much of a stretch to read a resurrection into Jesus' above words, remember that Jesus' enemies clearly understood what He was predicting. On the Saturday after Christ's crucifixion, the Jewish religious leaders met with the Roman procurator Pontius Pilate requesting help to secure Jesus' tomb. Why were they so desperate to make sure Jesus' tomb was sealed and guarded?

Now on the next day, the day after the preparation, the chief priests and the Pharisees gathered together with Pilate, and said, "Sir, we remember that when He was still alive that deceiver said, 'After three days I am to rise again.' Therefore, give orders for the grave to be made secure until the third day, otherwise His disciples may come and steal Him away and say to the people, 'He has risen from the dead,' and the last deception will be worse than the first." (Matthew 27:62–64)

Pilate acquiesced to their request to provide a guard unit because he, too, understood the severe ramifications of an empty tomb. Neither Pilate nor the religious leaders actually believed Jesus could conquer death, but they knew He had unequivocally claimed He would.

If the disciples faked Jesus' resurrection by stealing His body, Pilate and the Jewish leaders knew what would happen next. All of Jesus' followers would boast that He had fulfilled His own prophecy about a resurrection, which would prove Him to be the long-awaited Son of God. The Roman procurator and the Jewish religious leaders were determined to make sure *that* didn't happen.

Of course, Jesus' resurrection *did* happen and is proved by a mountain of evidence that we explored in the last chapter. But what is relevant to our current discussion is how Jesus' prophesied and actualized resurrection differentiates Him from any other religious leader or philosopher. No other religious leader or philosopher died in public, was buried in a guarded tomb, and rose again from the dead. And even if you are not sure that such a resurrection actually occurred, understand that no religious leader or philosopher even *claimed* he could conquer death, again demonstrating Jesus Christ's uniqueness.

Jesus claimed He would return to judge the world. Jesus also taught His followers that He would one day return to the earth to reward the righteous and to judge the unrighteous. No other religious leader or philosopher made such a grandiose claim. But Jesus did—frequently. In reference to Himself, Jesus said:

But when the Son of Man comes in His glory, and all the angels with Him, then he will sit on His glorious throne. All the nations will be gathered before Him; and He will separate them from one another, as the shepherd separates the sheep from the goats; and He will put the sheep on His right, and the goats on the left. (Matthew 25:31–33)

Do not marvel at this; for an hour is coming, in which all who are in the tombs will hear His voice, and will come forth; those who did the good deeds to a resurrection of life, those who committed the evil deeds to a resurrection of judgment. (John 5:28–29)

Here is another notable distinction between Jesus and other religious leaders. Some other faiths teach that a person's eternal destination is determined by worshipping the founder's god or obeying the founder's edicts. But Jesus taught that people's eternal destiny depended upon their acceptance or rejection of Jesus Himself as the Son of God:

For God did not send the Son into the world to judge the world, but that the world might be saved through Him. He who believes in Him is not judged; he who does not believe has been judged already, because he has not believed in the name of the only begotten Son of God. (John 3:17–18)

Therefore I said to you that you will die in your sins; for unless you believe that I am He, you will die in your sins. (John 8:24)

In his book *The World's Living Religions*, Robert Hume notes that all nine founders of the most popular non-Christian religions went through a period of uncertainty of their own identity or searching for spiritual light. But beginning at age twelve, Jesus evidenced a clear understanding of His identity and His life mission. Instead of searching for spiritual light like other leaders, Jesus claimed to be the Light of the World Himself (John 8:12).

These unique claims of Jesus present what some have termed a "trilemma" for people regarding Christ's identity, brilliantly summarized by C. S. Lewis:

I am trying here to prevent anyone saying the really foolish thing that people often say about Him: "I'm ready to accept Jesus as a great moral teacher, but I don't accept His claim to be god." That is the one thing we must not say.

A man who was merely a man and said the sort of things Jesus said would not be a great moral teacher. He would either be a lunatic—on a level with the man who says he is a poached egg—or else he would be the Devil of Hell.

You must make your choice. Either this man was, and is, the Son of God: or else a madman or something worse. You can shut him up for a fool, you can spit at Him and kill Him as a demon; or you can fall at His feet and call him Lord and God. But let us not come with any patronizing nonsense about His being a great human teacher. He has not left that open to us. He did not intend to.[16]

The Teaching of Jesus Christ

If you are not ready to label Jesus as a lunatic or a liar, then the only other possibility is that He was who He claimed to be: God in the flesh. If we conclude that Jesus is God, then we must also believe that everything Jesus said is true since God is incapable of deception (James 1:17; Hebrews 6:18). So, the natural question would be, did Jesus believe there are multiple paths to God? If Jesus is truly God, then He is obviously the most qualified Person in history to answer that question. What did Jesus have to say about this issue of exclusivity?

First, Jesus believed and taught that there are two possible eternal destinations for people after they die: heaven and hell: "These [the unrighteous] will go away into eternal punishment, but the righteous into eternal life" (Matthew 25:46). We will examine what Jesus taught about heaven and hell more extensively in chapter 5.

Not only did Jesus teach that there are two possible destinations for people when they die, but Jesus also observed that the majority of mankind chooses the wrong path that leads to the wrong destination. Jesus warned:

> Enter through the narrow gate; for the gate is wide and the way is broad that leads to destruction, and there are many who enter through it. For the gate is small and the way is narrow that leads to life, and there are few who find it. (Matthew 7:13–14)

Carefully consider how different Jesus' words are from the popular idea that everyone is on the same path, en route to the same spiritual destination or the notion that various religions represent different paths up the same mountain of truth. According to Jesus, there are only two spiritual paths: one leading to eternal life and another leading to eternal destruction. Alarmingly, among the "many" who are on the wide road leading to hell are religious people—some of whom claim to be followers of Jesus Christ:

> Not everyone who says to Me, "Lord, Lord," will enter the kingdom of heaven, but he who does the will of My Father who is in heaven will enter. Many will say to Me on that day, "Lord, Lord, did we not prophesy in your name, and in Your name cast out demons, and in Your name perform many miracles?" And then I will declare to them, "I never knew you; DEPART FROM ME, YOU WHO PRACTICE LAWLESSNESS." (Matthew 7:21–23)

Finally, Jesus believed that He offered the exclusive way for people to escape the horrors of hell and experience eternal life. When people accuse me of intolerance for suggesting that faith in Jesus Christ is the only way to experience heaven, I remind them that I am simply voicing what the Founder of our faith, Jesus, said: "I am the way, and the truth, and the life; no one comes to the Father but through Me" (John 14:6). I've never had anyone offer an effective rebuttal to Jesus' words—because there is none. He could not have been clearer.

As we have seen, Jesus taught that a person's eternal destiny depends on his decision to embrace or reject Christ's salvation: "Truly, truly I say to you, he who hears My word, and believes Him who sent Me, has eternal life, and does not come into judgment, but has passed out of death into life" (John 5:24). Sincere followers of other religions are not exempt from the requirement to trust in Christ alone for salvation.

I don't think it is accidental that Jesus chose to give His most detailed explanation about how to enter into heaven to a devout Jew rather than to a hardened atheist. Nicodemus is described as a "ruler of the Jews" (John 3:1), meaning that he was a member of the elite group of elders in Israel known as the Sanhedrin. He had spent his life trying to obey the Mosaic Law in order to please the one true God. If any religious belief system could have been an acceptable, alternate path leading to God it should have been Judaism.

Yet Jesus said even Judaism was incapable of offering eternal life to Nicodemus. In order to experience eternal life, Nicodemus had to be "born again" (John 3:3). Jesus then explained the only means by which a person could be spiritually reborn:

> As Moses lifted up the serpent in the wilderness, even so must the Son of Man be lifted up; so that *whoever believes* will in Him have eternal life. For God so loved the world, that He gave His only begotten Son, that *whoever believes in Him* shall not perish, but have eternal life. (John 3:14–16)

Some people argue that Jesus' death on the cross provides salvation for everyone, including those who embrace different religions. Yet notice the repetition in these verses of the phrase "whoever believes." Jesus never separated eternal salvation from personal belief.

Last spring I took a group to the Holy Land. Many who have made that journey will say that one of the most moving experiences is to sit in the Garden of Gethsemane and pray, just as Jesus did immediately before His arrest and crucifixion. He pleaded with God to allow Him to escape the horror of bearing the sins of the entire world and thereby experience something He had never experienced for one second of eternity past: separation from His heavenly Father.

In great anguish Jesus cried out, "Father, if You are willing, remove this cup from Me; yet not My will, but Yours be done" (Luke 22:42). But heaven was silent. God provided no other way to absolve mankind of our sin, because there *was* no other way. That is why Jesus insisted that He offered not just one path to God but the *only* path to God.

The Teaching of the New Testament

My friend Josh McDowell imagines a group of people traveling into a dense forest. As they get deeper into the forest they realize that they are lost. The group becomes fearful, understanding that their mistake may cost them their lives. However, as they peer into the distance they see a fork in the trail and two human forms at the fork in the road. The group runs toward these two people. When they arrive they notice that one has on a park uniform and is standing there perfectly healthy and alive. The other person is lying facedown, dead. Which person would you ask for directions to get out of the forest? Obviously, the one who is alive! McDowell writes, "When it comes to eternal matters, we are going to ask the one who is alive the way out of the predicament. This is not Mohammed, not Confucius, but Jesus Christ. Jesus is unique. He came back from the dead."[17]

Jesus' clear teaching that He provides the only way to heaven should be enough to settle the issue of exclusivity since He is the only religious leader who has conquered the problem of death. However, the New Testament writers affirm—both by teaching and illustrations—Jesus' declaration that faith in Him is the only means by which to escape eternal death.

Recently I was talking with a Jewish businessman in our city who laughed and said, "I'm surprised you are even talking with me since you Baptists think all of us Jews are going to hell because we don't accept Jesus." Smiling, I responded, "Well, we got that idea from the Jews!" His demeanor changed as he asked, "What do you mean?" I went on to explain that Jesus Christ claimed He was the only way to find salvation. "And Jesus was not a Southern Baptist evangelist, but a Jewish rabbi," I reminded my friend. In addition to Jesus, other devout followers of Judaism suddenly changed their belief system, embraced Christianity, and proclaimed that faith in Christ was the only path leading to salvation. The apostle Paul was a self-described "Hebrew of Hebrews" (Philippians 3:5) and a Pharisee, the strictest sect of Judaism known for its observance of the Mosaic Law. Paul's zeal for his Jewish faith led him to devote his life to stamping out the heresy claiming that Jesus of Nazareth was the long-awaited Messiah.

But while on his way to arrest a group of Christians in Damascus, Paul encountered the resurrected Jesus (Acts 9) and was suddenly transformed from the greatest antagonist of Christianity to the greatest evangelist for the Christian faith. After his experience with Christ, Paul longed to see his fellow Jews also embrace Christ as their Savior. In his letter to the Christians at Rome, Paul writes:

> Brethren, my heart's desire and my prayer to God for them [Israel] is for their salvation. . . . For not knowing about God's righteousness and seeking to establish their own, they did not subject themselves to the righteousness of God. For Christ is the end of the law for righteousness to everyone who believes. (Romans 10:1, 3–4)

Paul clearly believed that Jesus Christ was the only hope of salvation for all mankind, including his own people the Israelites. And he wasn't timid about making such a claim. "For I am not ashamed of the gospel, for it is the power of God for salvation to everyone who believes, to the Jew first and also to the Greek" (Romans 1:16).

Similarly, the apostle Peter had been a devout follower of Judaism until he became a disciple of Jesus Christ. After Christ's resurrection and ascension into heaven, Peter was willing to experience imprisonment, beatings, and ultimately execution for his faith in Christ. On one occasion, the Jewish leaders arrested Peter and a group of other disciples for preaching that Jesus Christ was the Messiah and healing a lame man by invoking the name of Jesus. "By what power, or in what name, have you done this?" the religious leaders demanded to know (Acts 4:7).

Peter didn't waver in his response:

Let it be known to all of you and to all the people of Israel, that by the name of Jesus Christ the Nazarene, whom you crucified, whom God raised from the dead—by this name this man stands here before you in good health. (Acts 4:10)

Peter could have qualified his statement by saying, "For this lame man, Jesus was the source of healing, but followers of other religions might call on a different name." But political correctness was not a concern for Peter. Instead, the apostle made it clear that faith in Jesus Christ provided the only means by which a person can escape the wrath of God:

There is salvation in no one else; for there is no other name under heaven that has been given among men by which we must be saved. (Acts 4:12)

Think about it. The three most prominent Jews in the New Testament—Jesus, the apostle Paul, and the apostle Peter—declared that no other religion (including Judaism) offered a road to heaven. Instead, the consistent message of the New Testament is that every person, regardless of his religious faith, is required to exercise personal faith in Jesus Christ for the forgiveness of sins.

One of the greatest illustrations of the exclusivity of Christianity is the conversion of a Roman centurion named Cornelius. Luke describes Cornelius as "a devout man and one who feared God with all his household, and gave many alms to the Jewish people and prayed to God continually" (Acts 10:2). Cornelius met all the criteria that the majority of people today believe qualify a person for heaven: he believed in God, he prayed to God regularly, and he possessed a healthy fear of God that motivated him to give money to the poor. And if those actions were not sufficient to merit entrance into heaven, Luke records that God actually communicated to Cornelius in a vision (v. 3).

But the message God communicated to Cornelius was that his worship of God and righteous deeds were insufficient for his salvation. Instead, God commanded Cornelius to send for the apostle Peter, who would communicate to the Roman centurion the message he needed to embrace in order to be saved. God orchestrated a series of miraculous events to bring Peter to Cornelius (not least of which was convincing Peter that non-Jews can be saved). When Peter finally met Cornelius he wasted no time in telling him the details of Jesus' life, death, and resurrection from the dead. In the climax of his message to Cornelius, Peter declared:

> He [Jesus] ordered us to preach to the people, and solemnly to testify that this is the One who has been appointed by God as Judge of the living and the dead. Of Him all the prophets bear witness that through His name everyone who believes in Him receives forgiveness of sins. (Acts 10:42–43)

Cornelius and those living in his house embraced the message of Jesus Christ and were saved and baptized that day (vv. 44–48).

I am often asked by people, "What about those who have never heard the gospel of Jesus Christ? Do you really believe God is going to send them to hell?" This story of Cornelius reminds us that when God sees someone who truly wants a relationship with Himself, He will move heaven and earth to make sure that person hears the message of Jesus Christ. However, this story also illustrates the truth that a person must hear and embrace the specific message of Jesus Christ in order to receive the forgiveness of his or her sins.

Cornelius' story is not unusual. The New Testament is filled with accounts of people like the followers of John the Baptist, an Ethiopian eunuch, the Jewish religious leader Nicodemus, and Paul's audience on Mars Hill who were told that their religious or philosophical beliefs could not lead them to eternal life. Just as the deity of Jesus Christ verifies the exclusive claims of Jesus Christ regarding salvation, the divine origin of the Bible (see chapter 2) gives credence to the New Testament claims that Christianity provides the only means of salvation.

THE UNIQUE SOLUTION TO MAN'S DILEMMA

All religions are not all wrong. C. S. Lewis writes in *Mere Christianity*, "if you are a Christian you do not have to believe that all the other religions are simply wrong all through. . . . If you are a Christian you are free to think that all these religions, even the queerest ones, contain some hint of the truth."[18] One of those truths about which many of the world religions agree is that mankind is riddled with selfish and destructive desires that lead him away from experiencing happiness in this life or in the afterlife (if that particular religion happens to believe in one).

However, all the major world religions, except for Christianity, posit that the solution to man's dilemma begins with man. For Eastern religions such as Hinduism and Buddhism, meditation is a solution that allows man to confront and conquer those destructive desires. Islam and Judaism are similar in that they require man to keep prescribed laws and follow religious rituals to appease their respective deities. Although Islam and Judaism have different laws and rituals, found in different religious books, in order to satisfy two different deities, they both teach the importance of human effort to satisfy their respective diety's requirements.

The impossibility of fulfilling the multitude of requirements each religion demands has led many followers to give up on complete obedience to their religions' standards. Reformed Jews and Muslims select those laws and rituals from their respective faiths they think are reasonable and possible to keep, and discard the rest. Perhaps they are hoping that God grades on a curve.

Like many other religions, Christianity also teaches that man's basic problem is internal. But the diagnosis of mankind's affliction is much more serious than other religions would have people believe. At the root of man's problem is his rebellion against his Creator. The Bible labels our innate hatred of God as "sin." Because man is infected with this spiritual virus, he is incapable of keeping all or even most of God's requirements. "For all of have sinned and fall short of the glory of God," Paul declares in Romans 3:23.

Furthermore, Christianity does not allow for selective obedience to God's requirements, as Paul reminds the Galatians who were trying to merit eternal life by keeping the law:

> For as many as are of the works of the Law are under a curse; for it is written, "CURSED IS EVERYONE WHO DOES NOT ABIDE BY ALL THINGS WRITTEN IN THE BOOK OF THE LAW, TO PERFORM THEM." (Galatians 3:10)

Remember when you were in school and loved those classes that were "pass/fail"? As long as you met the minimum requirements of the class, you were immune from the pressure of striving for a better grade. The Bible has some good news and bad news for all of us when it comes to our eternal destiny. The good news is that God utilizes the "pass/fail" system when judging us.

But the bad news is that if in a moment of weakness we fail to keep just one of God's requirements, it is as if we have failed to keep any of God's requirements. James wrote, "For whoever keeps the whole law and yet stumbles in one point, he has become guilty of all" (James 2:10). The penalty for such a failure is eternal separation from God. In demanding absolute perfection, the God of the Bible raises the performance requirements above that of any other religion or philosophy.

Our natural reaction to such a demand is, "No one can measure up to that kind of standard!" Exactly. Although some of us have failed to keep more of God's requirements than others, we nevertheless have all failed and are deserving of God's retribution. Man is in a helpless and hopeless situation from which he cannot escape.

But a loving God was able to do for us what we could never have done for ourselves. He formulated a plan by which He would endure the punishment we deserve for our transgressions so that we might experience an eternity in heaven with Him. When Jesus Christ died on that wooden cross more than two thousand years ago, He offered to take our sin so that we could receive His righteousness. The apostle Paul explained the greatest exchange in history this way:

[God] made Him [Jesus Christ] who knew no sin to be sin on our behalf, so that we might become the righteousness of God in Him. (2 Corinthians 5:21)

God offers to forgive us of our every failure to keep His laws on the basis of what Christ has done for us, not what we have done for Him. Unlike every other religion in the world, Christianity does not require that we earn God's favor in exchange for His forgiveness. It doesn't even allow for us to try.

> For by grace you have been saved through faith; and that not of yourselves, it is the gift of God; not a result of works, so that no one may boast. (Ephesians 2:8–9)

Many years ago during a British conference on world religions, experts were discussing the similarities and contrasts between the most popular faiths. Was there any concept truly unique to Christianity? During the heated debate, C. S. Lewis walked into the room. "What's the rumpus about?" the famous scholar asked. They explained they were discussing if there was anything unique about the Christian faith. "Oh, that's easy," Lewis replied. "It's grace."[19]

Every other religion has a long list of to-dos in order to merit whatever prize it may be offering. Only Christianity says that there are no to-dos because everything required for us to receive God's forgiveness for our sins has been *done* by God Himself. All we must do is receive the gift that God offers. Again, quoting C. S. Lewis, "Christ offers us something for nothing. He even offers everything for nothing. In a sense the whole Christian life consists in accepting that very remarkable offer."[20]

And perhaps that is the strongest argument for Christianity being the right religion. Christianity provides an exclusive answer to man's greatest dilemma, expressed by Job when he asked, "How can a man be in the right before God?" (Job 9:2). Every other religion answers that question with "work." Only Christianity answers "grace."

CHAPTER FOUR

HOW CAN I KNOW GOD IS GOOD WITH ALL THE SUFFERING IN THE WORLD?

B art Ehrman was a card-carrying evangelical Christian by anyone's standards. He was baptized in a Congregational church and reared as an Episcopalian. However, when he was a teenager attending a Youth for Christ meeting Ehrman was "born again" through his personal faith in Jesus Christ. Sensing God's call into ministry, Ehrman decided to attend the ultraconservative Moody Bible Institute in Chicago for his training. During this period in his life he memorized entire books of the New Testament and graduated from Moody with a degree in Bible and theology.

He finished his college studies at Wheaton College, which at the time was another renowned bastion of evangelical Christianity. While at Wheaton, Ehrman studied Greek so that he could read the New Testament in its original language and later earned both a Masters of Divinity and a Doctor of Philosophy degree in New Testament studies at Princeton Theological Seminary. During Ehrman's time in college and seminary he served as a youth minister and eventually pastor of a Baptist church.

By Erhman's own account, it was during this period of time that he began to lose his faith and, by his own admission, today no longer considers himself to be a Christian. His departure from Christianity began with his doubts about the divine inspiration of the Bible as re-counted in his book *Misquoting Jesus* (it is interesting how almost every defection from Christianity begins with doubts about the trustworthi-ness of Scripture).

But the tipping point for Erhman's defection from Christianity was his inability to reconcile the evil in the world with the existence of the loving and all-powerful God portrayed in the Bible:

> I realized that I could no longer reconcile the claims of faith with the facts of life. In particular, I could no longer explain how there can be a good and all-powerful God actively involved with this world, given the state of things. For many people who inhabit this planet, life is a cesspool of misery and suffering. I came to a point where I simply could not believe that there is a good and kindly disposed Ruler who is in charge of it.
>
> The problem of suffering became for me the problem of faith. . . . I don't "know" if there is a God; but I think that if there is one, he certainly isn't the one proclaimed by the Judeo-Christian tradi-tion, the one who is actively and powerfully involved in this world. And so, I stopped going to church.[1]

ANOTHER PERSPECTIVE

Vicky Olivas was not excited about having to find a job, but her hus-band's desire for a divorce left her no choice. She had to support herself and her two-year-old child. One bright Friday morning, Vicky went for a job interview in a factory district in Los Angeles. She walked into the dimly lit front office and found no one. She continued down the hallway and eventually discovered two men seated behind a desk in the warehouse. After some introductions, the man who appeared to be the boss directed Vicky back to the front office to fill out an application.

While she completed the forms, the boss entered the room and closed and locked the door. He grabbed her around the chest and threw her against the wall. "I asked them to send somebody just like you," he said as he grabbed at her blouse. Vicky was trying to push him away when she heard the gunshot. She slumped to the floor, feeling the warm blood trickling down her neck. Her assailant dragged her to a car and dumped her at the emergency room at a nearby hospital. She was completely paralyzed.

Her attacker was eventually arrested, having been convicted of rape three times previously. After serving three years in jail, he was released. Vicky Olivas, innocent of any crime, was sentenced to a lifetime of suffering in a wheelchair. Unlike Bart Erhman, who only wrestled with theories about evil from a philosopher's chair, Vicky Olivas struggled every day with the gritty realities of evil. How did such a cruel injustice affect her faith in Christ? In a note to a friend, Vicky wrote,

> I'm being prepared to touch the wonderful scarred hands of our Lord. To know that I'm sharing with Christ in suffering is really uplifting and comforting. I can truly say that my "wheelchair" is a gift from God and that earth can never meet my deepest longings, only Christ can. I want to throw off all that hinders my path to heaven. When I meet Jesus face to face, I want to have as much tangible proof as I can to show him that I love Him and have been faithful. Our journey has been a difficult one, and for as long as the Lord has us here on this earth, it will continue to be hard. But what an honor to suffer for Him.[2]

Two professing followers of Jesus Christ collide with the reality of suffering. One is driven away from God, while the other is drawn into a closer relationship with her Creator. While the outcomes are different, there is one point of similarity from both stories. Everyone who confronts suffering personally or even philosophically is forced to grapple with disturbing questions.

THE TUNNEL OF CHAOS

The senior staff of our church has been working with a consulting group to help us strategize about the future ministry plan for our congregation. The consultants recently led our staff through a session they called "The Tunnel of Chaos," during which they challenged our core assumptions about our church's worship style, our target audience, and our definition of success in ministry. Some of the staff stumbled out of the session dazed and confused. Some of their most basic beliefs had been turned upside down.

Anyone who comes face-to-face with the reality of evil and suffering in the world enters his own "tunnel of chaos" that can either strengthen or destroy his most fundamental beliefs about God. Author Lee Strobel cites a national survey that asked a cross-section of American adults, "If you could ask God only one question and you knew he would give you an answer, what would you ask?" The top response was, "Why is there pain and suffering in the world?"[3] It is a question that believers, unbelievers, and doubters have to confront at some point in their lives.

Why does the existence of evil and suffering in the world pose such a problem for people's belief in God? I've never heard anyone ask, "How can I know there is a God with all of the porcupines in the world?" The existence of porcupines does not challenge the existence of God. Both realities are compatible. However, it is very difficult for us to reconcile these four truths:

1. God exists.
2. God is all-powerful.
3. God is good.
4. Evil is present in the world.

Philosopher David Hume's famous trilemma about God's goodness, God's power, and evil has troubled many: "Is God willing to prevent evil, but not able? Then he is impotent. Is he able, but not willing? Then he is malevolent. Is he both able and willing? Whence then is evil?"[4] According to Hume, the reality of evil gives us only three alternatives about God: He is impotent, He is evil, or He is nonexistent.

I learned a long time ago about the dangers of limiting your options in debating. During a logic and argumentation class in college I was using the story of God's command to Joshua to destroy every living being in Ai as a referendum on the inerrancy of the Bible, claiming, "You only have two options: either God said it, or He didn't say it." My professor replied, "No, Mr. Jeffress, there is a third option. Maybe God said it, and He was just kidding!"

RECONCILING THE REALITY OF SUFFERING AND GOD'S EXISTENCE

There is another option for the Hume trilemma that we will discover later. But first, let's look at some common approaches to reconciling the reality of suffering with the possibility of God's existence.

Explanation #1: "Suffering Is an Illusion"

Some would argue that suffering is a perception rather than a reality. Mary Baker Eddy, the founder of the Christian Science Movement, writes:

> Christian Science raises the standard of liberty and cries: "Follow me! Escape the bondage of sickness, sin, and death!" . . . The illusion of material sense, not divine law, has bound you, entangled your free limbs, crippled your capacities, enfeebled your body, and defaced the tablet of your being. . . . If sickness and sin are illusions, the awakening from this mortal dream, or illusion, will bring us into health, holiness, and immortality.[5]

Sin, sickness, and death are nothing but illusions, Eddy taught. "If sin, sickness, and death were understood as nothingness, they would disappear," she claimed.[6] Yet her life experiences reveal that she did not even believe her own claims. While Eddy was sick, her doctors reported that they administered medicine to her. Just before her death, Eddy apparently arranged for a woman who resembled her to sit in her carriage and be driven to her house in order to deceive Eddy's followers into believing she was well.

The reality of suffering can neither be denied nor minimized. Many years ago I was in my office in the church I was serving in West Texas. My secretary buzzed me and said a man wanted to see me. During our conversation he related to me how a Sunday in June 1980 forever changed his life. On that particular Sunday morning, he and his family were worshipping in church. Everyone in the congregation was excited about the first Sunday of their new pastor. The auditorium was packed. A visitor entered through the back door carrying a gun and yelled, "This is war!" He opened fire on the congregation, killing five people and wounding twelve others. The man in my office said he was seated next to his seven-year-old daughter when the gunshots hit her. She died instantly.

At the funeral service several days later, the father could not bear to say good-bye to his daughter. Finally, the pastor came over and told the father, "It's time to go; the cemetery workers will cover the grave." The dad was so filled with sorrow over the loss of his daughter and remorse over time not spent with her that he took off his coat and tie and grabbed a shovel, saying, "The least I can do for my daughter is to cover her grave."

Unfortunately, the story did not end there. He and the other families who lost loved ones that day spent eighteen months trying to bring the gunman to trial. They learned that the killer had been convicted of molesting his own daughter but had been released on a technicality.

Can you imagine trying to comfort that grieving father by saying, "The pain you are feeling isn't real; it is only an illusion" or "Evil doesn't really exist; it is only a matter of perception"? Evil in the world—and the resulting suffering we experience—is very real and very painful. Fortunately, the Bible does not deny or minimize either reality.

For we know that the whole creation groans and suffers the pains of childbirth together until now. And not only this, but also we ourselves, having the first fruits of the Spirit, even we ourselves groan within ourselves, waiting eagerly for our adoption as sons, the redemption of our body. (Romans 8:22–23)

These things I [Jesus] have spoken to you, so that in Me you may have peace. In the world you have tribulation, but take courage; I have overcome the world. (John 16:33)

We are afflicted in every way, but not crushed; perplexed, but not despairing; persecuted, but not forsaken; struck down, but not destroyed; always carrying about in the body the dying of Jesus, so that the life of Jesus also may be manifested in our body. (2 Corinthians 4:8–10)

One powerful argument for the trustworthiness of the Bible is that it does not sugarcoat reality like other religious writings. Life is filled with pain. Suffering is only an illusion to those who have not experienced it.

Explanation #2: "The God of the Bible Does Not Exist"

Many people are uncomfortable stating categorically that there is no higher power in the universe. But if such a force exists, they think, it certainly could not be the God described in the Bible. How could a God who claims to be the embodiment of love, a hater of evil, and an all-powerful deity allow atrocities like floods, famines, torture, and genocide? If suffering and evil are real, then it must be God who is the illusion, according to this explanation.

Steve Jobs, the cofounder of Apple, died at the age of fifty-six. Although he was a fan of Eastern philosophy, there was a time early in his life when his adoptive parents took him to a traditional Christian church. One Sunday when Jobs was thirteen, he brought a copy of the July 1968 edition of *Life* magazine to church. The cover showed a pair of starving children in Biafra. Jobs confronted the church's pastor with the highly disturbing photograph.

"If I raise my finger, will God know which one I'm going to raise even before I do it?" Jobs asked. The pastor answered, "Yes, God knows everything." Jobs then pointed to the *Life* cover and asked, "Well, does God know about this and what's going to happen to those children?" The pastor replied, "Steve, I know you don't understand, but yes, God knows about that." Dissatisfied with the pastor's explanation, Steve Jobs walked out of the church that day, never to return.[7]

The pastor could have said to Jobs, "I know you are deeply disturbed by the reality of starving children. But ask yourself, 'Why do I care about this?' The fact that you are angry about evil and suffering in the world argues strongly for the existence of a good and loving God." Had Jobs been intrigued enough by the pastor's claim to have hung around a little longer, the pastor might have continued this way: "Nothing can be labeled 'evil' without a beginning reference point for what is 'good.' A line that is described as 'crooked' assumes the objective standard of 'straight.'

"In the same way, there must be a universal moral standard by which we determine that starvation, slavery, genocide, and rape are evil, rather than a matter of personal preference. If there is a universal moral standard by which all behavior is measured, then there must be a divine Being who constructed that moral ruler and placed it in every human heart."

When Christian apologist Ravi Zacharias was confronted by an angry student about the supposed impossibility of reconciling evil in the world with the existence of God, Zacharias answered,

> If there is such a thing as evil, aren't you assuming there is such a thing as good? [And] when you accept the existence of goodness, you must affirm a moral law on the basis of which to differentiate between good and evil. But when you admit to a moral law, you must posit a moral lawgiver. For if there is no moral lawgiver, there is no moral law. If there is no moral law, there is no good. If there is no good, there is no evil. What, then, is your question?[8]

The fact that there is evil in the world—and that we care about it—argues strongly for the existence of a good God.

Explanation #3: "God Is Limited"

If you believe in the existence of a loving God (as opposed to a sadistic Creator who enjoys inflicting pain upon His creatures—a possibility that few want to contemplate) and the reality of suffering, then divine castration seems to be an easy way to reconcile the two realities. God sees the pain you are experiencing, He weeps over your distress, and He offers comfort in your affliction. Yet He is ultimately powerless to stop your pain. "Open theism," "process theology," and "finite godism" are some of the theories used to strip God of His sovereignty (His rule over His creation), omniscience (His knowledge of what is happening and what will happen in the future), and omnipotence (His power).

Rabbi Harold Kushner's loss of his young son caused him to conclude that "even God has a hard time keeping chaos in check and limiting the damage that evil can do."[9] Why can't God keep evil under control? Kushner explains, "I recognize His limitations. He is limited in what He can do by the laws of nature and by the evolution of human nature and human moral freedom."[10] As one Jewish writer said after reading Kushner's book, "If that's who God is, why doesn't he resign and let someone more competent take his place?"[11]

Have the laws of nature limited God's power? God reminded Job that He is the One who is in control over the natural world and the One who established the boundaries that govern the natural world:

> Where were you when I laid the foundation of the earth? Tell me, if you have understanding, who set its measurements? Since you know. Or who stretched the line on it? On what were its bases sunk? Or who laid its cornerstone, when the morning stars sang together and all the sons of God shouted for joy?
>
> Or who enclosed the sea with doors when, bursting forth, it went out from the womb? . . .
>
> Have you ever in your life commanded the morning, and caused the dawn to know its place, that it might take hold of the ends of the earth, and the wicked be shaken out of it? (Job 38:4–8, 12–13)

God spends three chapters declaring to Job that He controls nature; nature does not control God. The laws God has established to govern the operation of the natural world do not in any way limit His ability to override those laws. For example, in the church I lead I have established policies for the staff that I expect them to follow. One of those policies is that we do not have events on Saturday night that would detract from Sunday morning. However, the junior high minister recently asked me for permission to have a lock-in for students on a Saturday night with the promise that they would be in church Sunday. I granted him an exception to the policy (just as long as I didn't have to attend!).

Since God established the principles that govern the operation of His creation, He has the freedom to override those principles. Just imagine all of the physical laws God suspended for the parting of the Red Sea, the virgin birth of Christ, the feeding of the five thousand, and the resurrection of Jesus Christ from the dead!

Rabbi Kushner and others also claim that God's power is limited by human freedom. God is incapable of preventing, or even knowing beforehand, what people are going to do, they claim. Clark Pinnock writes, "The future is really open and not available to exhaustive fore-knowledge even on the part of God. It is plain that the biblical doctrine of creaturely freedom requires us to reconsider the conventional wisdom of the omniscience of God."[12]

In other words, God would like to stop a rapist from attacking an elderly woman but is incapable of doing so for two reasons, according to those who believe in a finite god. First, God did not know ahead of time what the rapist would do, meaning that the futures of both the rapist and the woman were "open" rather than planned before their births. Second, even if God could have known what the rapist would do, He was helpless to stop him because of the rapist's free will.

The claim that God had no foreknowledge of the rapist's actions and the woman's future contradicts the testimony of Scripture. David writes that every detail of every day of our life was written in God's book before we lived one of those days:

> Your eyes have seen my unformed substance; and in Your book were all written the days that were ordained for me, when as yet there was not one of them. (Psalm 139:16)

Additionally, God not only knows what His creatures will do, but He also maintains authority over His creatures. Perhaps this illustration will help. As pastor of our church, I have a great deal of freedom: I choose what sermons to preach, what staff to hire, and when to come in and leave every day. Yet I have that freedom only because the congregation that called me as pastor chooses to vest that authority in me. At any moment the congregation could call a meeting and dismiss me as pastor. In a Baptist church, the congregation gives and the congregation can take away. Just because the congregation hasn't dismissed me yet doesn't mean that they approve of every decision I have made. I continue to have freedom . . . until I no longer have freedom.

Similarly, any freedom we have to make choices originates with God. When Pontius Pilate threatened Jesus with the power he had to either free Him or crucify Him, Jesus reminded Pilate, "You would have no power over me if it were not given to you from above" (John 19:11 NIV). However, any freedom we have been granted by God in no way diminishes God's power over us. The Bible is filled with examples of God thwarting the plans of people. For example, the Jewish leaders, infuriated by the teaching of Jesus, sought to kill Him:

> They were seeking to seize Him; and no man laid his hand on Him, because His hour had not yet come. (John 7:30)

Why were Jesus' enemies unable to kill Him prematurely? John does not tell us whether God changed their hearts or changed Jesus' circumstances, allowing for His miraculous escape. Either way, the Jewish leaders' original desire to take Jesus' life was circumvented.

But other passages of Scripture teach that God's rule extends over the desires and intentions of a person's heart:

> So then [God] has mercy on whom He desires, and He hardens whom He desires. (Romans 9:18)

Human beings are free . . . until they are not free. We will explore the mystery of the relationship between God's sovereignty and our responsibility further in the next section. Nevertheless, when confronted with difficult problems such as reconciling the existence of suffering with the goodness of God, we need to remember it is much easier to lower our view of God than to raise our faith to trust in God's goodness and wisdom.

Even my logic and argumentation professor from college—who was not particularly bent toward the spiritual—would see that there is at least one other option for reconciling the reality of suffering with the existence of an all-powerful and loving God. But before we look at that alternative, it is important to understand something about those who ask for help in reconciling suffering with the existence of God.

In my thirty-plus years of ministry, I have come to realize that most people who challenge the existence of God because of suffering are not so much concerned with suffering in the world at large as they are with suffering in their own lives. Usually there is some deep hurt—the death of a friend or family member, sexual abuse, betrayal—that causes them to question the existence of God. Their deep emotional wounds cannot be healed by cold, philosophical explanations alone.

When people who are hurting challenge you to defend the existence of a good God, I encourage you to begin the discussion by demonstrating genuine concern about their situation. Assure them that God—as distant or nonexistent as He may feel—is distressed over their distress. "The Lord is close to those whose hearts are breaking," the psalmist assures us (Psalm 34:18 TLB). Most of all, admit that you don't have the complete answer to the question "Why did God allow this to happen to me?" Then consider using this illustration.

One night my wife and I were traveling on an interstate highway in the middle of West Texas in a driving rainstorm when our headlights went out due to an electrical malfunction in our car. We could not see two inches in front of us, but we were hesitant to pull over to the shoulder of the road for fear of being hit by another car. Thankfully, we spotted an eighteen-wheeler in our rear-view mirror. We allowed it to pass us and then we simply zeroed in on its taillights and followed it safely into the city limits of our town.

God's Word is described as a "light to [our] path" (Psalm 119:105) that provides direction, especially when we lose our way in the fog of pain, suffering, and the unrelenting storm of doubt. Although there is no specific chapter-and-verse answer in the Bible to "Why does God allow suffering in the world?" the Bible does offer some truths we can depend on to lead us safely through storms that blow into our lives.

GOD IS BOTH GOOD AND ALL-POWERFUL

Admittedly, it is difficult to reconcile God's absolute control over His creation with His inherent goodness. Just this morning I read the horrifying account of a father who murdered his wife and then, fearing his two little boys would tell the police, used a hatchet to murder them before setting them on fire. If we accept the existence of God and the reality of evil, then we must conclude that a God who would allow such an atrocity is either evil or impotent. Yet neither conclusion is a viable alternative.

Both biblical and natural revelation attest to the goodness of God who is defined by His love for righteousness and hatred of evil:

Then the LORD passed by in front of [Moses] and proclaimed, "The LORD, the LORD God, compassionate and gracious, slow to anger, and abounding in lovingkindness and truth." (Exodus 34:6)

Far be it from God to do wickedness, and from the Almighty to do wrong. (Job 34:10)

Good and upright is the LORD. (Psalm 25:8)

O taste and see that the LORD is good; how blessed is the man who takes refuge in Him! (Psalm 34:8)

The earth is full of Your lovingkindness, O Lᴏʀᴅ. (Psalm 119:64)

Fᴏʀ ᴛʜᴇ ᴇʏᴇs ᴏꜰ ᴛʜᴇ Lᴏʀᴅ ᴀʀᴇ ᴛᴏᴡᴀʀᴅ ᴛʜᴇ ʀɪɢʜᴛᴇᴏᴜs, ᴀɴᴅ Hɪs ᴇᴀʀs ᴀᴛᴛᴇɴᴅ ᴛᴏ ᴛʜᴇɪʀ ᴘʀᴀʏᴇʀ, ʙᴜᴛ ᴛʜᴇ ꜰᴀᴄᴇ ᴏꜰ ᴛʜᴇ Lᴏʀᴅ ɪs ᴀɢᴀɪɴsᴛ ᴛʜᴏsᴇ ᴡʜᴏ ᴅᴏ ᴇᴠɪʟ. (1 Peter 3:12)

The one who does not love does not know God, for God is love. (1 John 4:8)

Obviously, using the Bible to argue the goodness of God assumes the truthfulness of Scripture. Yet, even apart from the Bible, the world is filled with evidence of a benevolent Creator. Yes, occasionally floods and earthquakes kill thousands of people, but most of the time rivers stay within their banks and the tectonic plates do not shift. Farmers periodically struggle with droughts that destroy their crops, but usually sufficient rains come that protect their livelihood and provide our food. We read of unspeakable crimes committed against people, forgetting the reason they are reported is that such crimes are the exception rather than the rule. The outpouring of financial support for those whose lives are destroyed by natural disasters and the selfless work of those trying to assist those living in poverty are reflections of the goodness of God, in whose image we are made.

The Old Testament patriarch Job certainly had his reasons for questioning the goodness of God after losing his children, his possessions, and his health. Although Job struggled with reconciling God's goodness and power with his predicament, he realized early on the weakness of the argument that suffering is prima facie evidence against God. When Job's wife advised him to "Curse God and die!" Job asked, "Shall we indeed accept good from God and not accept adversity?" (Job 2:9–10). Job understood that if evil in the world is evidence against God, then goodness in the world must be evidence for God.

The reason we are surprised, upset, and confused by natural disasters, illnesses, and crimes is that such calamities are the exception rather than the norm. But even if all the good things we experience in life were negated by an equal amount of bad things, one could not logically use those difficulties to disprove the existence of a loving God. The case for a benevolent, all-powerful God would be just as strong as the case against such a God.

"But, Robert," you may protest, "if God hates evil as much as the Bible claims, why doesn't He intervene and put an end to evil and suffering in the world?" As noted earlier, some have tried to answer the question by limiting God's power over circumstances or people. When a mate walks out of a marriage, when the doctor's report shows a malignancy, or when a child is killed in a car crash, some people try to comfort themselves with the thought that *God loves me and would have stopped this from happening had He been able.*

But does belief in a God with limited power offer any real hope? Author Steve Farrar writes that those who attempt to limit God's control over His creation have "stripped off the bark of God's sovereignty and thrown it in the dumpster. The worldly equivalent would be a park ranger peeling the two feet of bark off a giant sequoia. When the bark has been stripped, you have absolutely no protection when a fire comes raging into your life."[13]

When—not if—the fire of adversity comes raging into your life, the only protection you have is the assurance that there is a God surrounding you who controls both the intensity and direction of the fire. Otherwise, you and I are nothing more than victims of random events.

Do you find any comfort in the thought that any one of the trillions of cells in your body could randomly start to multiply on its own, or that your employer could arbitrarily choose to fire you, or a distracted driver could accidentally take the life of your loved one while a less-than-sovereign God stood by, helpless to intervene? Fortunately, the Bible assures us of God's absolute control over all His creation:

O Lord, the God of our fathers, are You not God in the heavens? And are You not ruler over all the kingdoms of the nations? Power and might are in Your hand so that no one can stand against You. (2 Chronicles 20:6)

The Lord has established His throne in the heavens, and His sovereignty rules over all. (Psalm 103:19)

I know that the Lord is great and that our Lord is above all gods. Whatever the Lord pleases, He does, in heaven and in earth, in the seas and in all deeps. (Psalm 135:5–6)

The great nineteenth-century preacher Charles Haddon Spurgeon believed that God's control of His universe extended to the minutest of details:

I believe that every particle of dust that dances in the sunbeam does not move an atom more or less than God wishes, that every particle of spray that dashes against the steamboat has its orbit as well as the sun in the heavens, that the chaff from the hand of the winnower is steered as the stars in their courses, that the creeping of an aphid over a rosebud is as much fixed as the march of the devastating pestilence, and the fall of the sere leaves from the poplar is as fully ordained as the tumbling of an avalanche. He who believes in God must believe in this truth.[14]

Does it make sense that a God who guides every detail of the natural world with such precision would adopt a hands-off approach when it comes to His crowning work of creation: mankind? God's control over His creation extends into every detail of your life as well. As one pastor said, "There is no will or act of creatures, men, angels, or demons that can do other than work for our good. No dog can bark against us, no man can act or speak against us . . . the Law of Gravity cannot cause anything to fall on us unless it has first been sifted through the will of God."[15]

Admittedly, God's absolute control over His creation brings up many questions—some of which can be answered and many that cannot. As Chuck Swindoll says, the sovereignty of God "does not take away my questions, but it does relieve me of my anxiety."[16]

EVIL IS NOT
ATTRIBUTABLE TO GOD

Author John Ortberg writes about a woman he knows named Sheryl who went into a beauty salon to have her nails manicured. The beautician said, "I don't believe God exists." Sheryl asked her why, and the beautician responded, "Well, you just have to go out on the street to realize God doesn't exist. Tell me, if God exists would there be so many sick people? Would there be abandoned children? If God existed, there would be neither suffering nor pain. I can't imagine a loving God who could allow these things."

Sheryl offered no rebuttal and simply left the shop when her nails were finished. Immediately after exiting the beauty shop she saw a woman in the street with long, stringy, dirty hair. Sheryl went back into the beauty shop and announced to the beautician, "You know what? Beauticians do not exist." "How can you say that? I am here. I just worked on you," the beautician said. "No," Sheryl countered. "Beauticians do not exist because if they did, there would be no people with dirty, long hair and appearing very unkempt like that woman outside." The beautician protested, "Beauticians do exist. The problem is, people don't come to me."[17] Bingo!

One of the maxims of leadership is "He who calls the shots, takes the shots." However, many times the criticism leaders must endure is unfounded. That certainly is true when it comes to the tendency we have to use the existence of suffering and evil in the world to accuse

God or deny God. The blame for most everything we describe as "evil" in the world around us can be laid at the feet of man, not God. Let me explain.

Theologians categorize evil as either natural evil (earthquakes, famines, and tsunamis) or moral evil (genocide, terrorism, or injustice). The Bible teaches that both natural and moral evil in the world are the result of man's rebellion against God. As a result of Adam's and Eve's original sin, God declared, "Cursed is the ground because of you" (Genesis 3:17). This judgment against creation involved more than God making Adam work harder to grow produce out of the ground. The apostle Paul explains that the ramifications of man's first sin extended to all of the created order:

> For the creation was subjected to futility, not willingly, but because of Him who subjected it, in hope that the creation itself also will be set free from its slavery to corruption into the freedom of the glory of the children of God. For we know that the whole creation groans and suffers the pains of childbirth together until now. (Romans 8:20–22)

The "futility" to which God subjected the world is the tendency that all systems have to move toward disorder, as described by the second law of thermodynamics. The resulting "groans" of that disorder and disintegration of all systems in nature are manifested in everything from earthquakes to the aches and pains of old age. While it is true that God is ultimately responsible for these consequences, it is also true that this disorder and disintegration in the natural world is directly attributable to man's rebellion against God.

Similarly, all of the moral evils in the world are traceable to man, not to God. As C. S. Lewis observes, most of the evil in the world has been produced by human beings with "whips, guns, bayonets, gas chambers and bombs."[18] Think about the great atrocities committed against human beings in history by Nazi Germany, Communist China, and Communist Russia. By some estimates, these regimes slaughtered more than one hundred million people. Were these regimes known for their abiding faith in God? No, it was their disbelief in a Creator that produced the moral vacuum in which such unspeakable crimes against humanity could occur.

Some would respond by saying, "Even though God is not directly responsible for such evil, the fact that He doesn't stop evil makes Him culpable." Author Dinesh D'Souza uses the illustration of the shooter who massacred thirty-two students at Virginia Tech in 2007. Obviously, God is not the one who pulled the trigger, directly causing the students to die. But He certainly had the power to stop the shooter by jamming the gun or even striking the gunman dead. Why didn't God intervene?

D'Souza offers one explanation: perhaps God knew that such a tragedy would draw people to Himself. Seeing the reality of good and evil through such a horrible crime drives some people toward their Creator. Of course, some people react violently to such a suggestion. "Are you claiming that God would murder innocent students in order to cause other people to worship Him?" But remember, God is not the One directly responsible for the killings. "Blame guns, blame the school's security system, most of all blame the killer himself, but don't blame God."[19]

Still, some would counter that God's unwillingness to stop the shooter makes Him indirectly responsible for the massacre. After all, if you see a child being abducted in broad daylight and have the power to stop the kidnapper and don't, you bear some responsibility for the abduction. Similarly, God's unwillingness to stop the shooter at Virginia Tech means that He must bear some responsibility for the tragedy, doesn't it?

It is important at this point to reaffirm the sovereignty of God over all His creation. Could God have stopped the killer by changing his heart or jamming his gun? Absolutely! Does He sometimes supernaturally override the sinful intentions of those who would seek to harm others? Most definitely, as illustrated earlier in the life of Jesus. But if God were continually thwarting every desire people had to rebel against Him, then there would be no such thing as true righteousness in the world. In a world in which God supernaturally prevented evil "human goodness would be mere programming, not goodness."[20]

God has given human beings the freedom to obey or disobey His divine decrees. While theologians will continue to argue the extent of that freedom, the bottom line is that God does not coerce anyone to obey Him. Apologist Norman Geisler writes, "Since God is love, he cannot force himself on anyone against his will. Forced love is not love; it is rape. And God is not a divine rapist."[21] Where freedom exists there will always be the possibility of evil.

GOD CAN USE SUFFERING FOR GOOD

Suffering is often a matter of perspective in God's creation. For example, the earthquakes and tsunamis that make headlines and prompt the question "Why would God allow such catastrophes to occur?" are the result of plate tectonics under the surface of the earth and ocean floor. Peter Ward and Donald Brownlee point out in their book *Rare Earth* that our planet is apparently the only one that has these plate tectonics.

While plate tectonics occasionally produce natural disasters, they are also essential for the biodiversity that allows life to flourish on our planet. These plate tectonics regulate our climate and keep the earth's land from being submerged in water. Could God have created a world not reliant on plate tectonics? Yes, the authors concede, life could exist without plate tectonics, but not with human beings like you and I.[22]

Many times our lack of complete information causes us to prematurely judge something that is painful as "evil." While we use the terms "suffering" and "evil" interchangeably, perhaps this is the time to decouple the two terms. They are not the same. Everything that is evil does not always result in suffering (at least in the short term) and everything that produces suffering is not always evil.

For example, if you did not know anything about surgery and walked into a hospital operating room in the middle of a heart transplant, what would you think? You would see a person strapped to a gurney, while in horror you would see a masked man with a drill opening up his chest cavity and reaching in and removing a beating heart. Would you not conclude that you were watching the torture of an innocent victim? Only if you stayed around long enough to see another heart placed in the patient and the patient awakened and gratified by the new life he had been given would you have a complete picture of what you had just witnessed.

Our world is replete with examples of pain as a precursor to good. Pain is a tutor that instructs children not to touch a hot stove. It is through the pain of childbirth that new life enters the world. Pain can alert both the patient and the doctor to the presence of a malignancy that needs to be removed. Therefore, we should not be surprised by the claim that God can use temporary suffering for ultimate good.

For example, consider the experience of the Old Testament character Joseph. His brothers, filled with jealously over his favorite-son status with his father, sold him into slavery. Yet through a miraculous set of circumstances, God used the brothers' betrayal to place Joseph in Egypt where he would become prime minister of this powerful nation. When a famine struck Egypt and Canaan, Joseph's position allowed him to provide food for his brothers and therefore preserve the nucleus of what would become the nation of Israel—the nation from which the Savior of the world would be born.

When Joseph was reunited with his brothers he reflected on how God had used his brothers' treacherous act for a greater good: "As for you, you meant evil against me, but God meant it for good in order to bring about this present result, to preserve many people alive" (Genesis 50:20). Notice that Joseph did not make this great pronouncement when his brothers were selling him like an animal to the Ishmaelites: "What you guys are doing is wrong, but God is bigger than you and is somehow going to use this for good." It was not until decades later that Joseph was able to look back and see how God used an inherently evil action to achieve His purpose.

The ultimate example of God's ability to use suffering (and even blatant evil) to accomplish good is in the death of Jesus Christ. When you think about it, Jesus Christ represents the only truly innocent person who has ever suffered. The rest of us human beings are all guilty of *something*.

When His lifeless body was removed from the cross on that Friday afternoon (no one was calling it Good Friday at that point), it looked as if evil had triumphed over good. Even Jesus Himself, in full expression of His humanity, cried out moments before His death, "MY GOD, MY GOD, WHY HAVE YOU FORSAKEN ME?" (Matthew 27:46).

But the passing of several days and an empty tomb provided a different perspective from which to evaluate the greatest injustice in human history. God was able to use the evil acts of the Jewish and Roman leaders to accomplish His ultimate purpose of rescuing all creation from the vice grip of sin. Shortly after Christ's resurrection and ascension into heaven, the apostle Peter addressed many of those who had been responsible for Jesus' death:

This Man [Jesus], delivered over by the predetermined plan and foreknowledge of God, you nailed to a cross by the hands of godless men and put Him to death. (Acts 2:23)

In that simple statement lies an unfathomable mystery. Godless men with nothing but evil intentions were directly responsible for

Christ's death. Yet God not only knew this terrible injustice would occur; He actually planned it! It is beyond my pay grade to understand how a holy God could use evil to accomplish His perfect plan. But one truth is obvious: God is always at work accomplishing His ultimate plan. In his book *Mystery of the Cross*, Alister McGrath writes:

> Experience cannot be allowed to have the final word—it must be judged and shown up as deceptive and misleading. The theology of the Cross draws our attention to the sheer unreliability of experience as a guide to the presence and activity of God. God is active and present in his world, quite independently of whether we experience him as being so. Experience declared that God was absent from Calvary, only to have its verdict humiliatingly overturned on the third day.[23]

We must resist the impulse we have either to accuse or deny God when we are in the tunnel of chaos that comes from suffering. When in that dark tunnel it is difficult to see anything, especially God. Only when we emerge from that tunnel into the daylight can we make a more informed decision about what we have experienced. As a pastor, I cannot begin to count how many times I have listened to people who have endured bankruptcy, suffered the breakup of a marriage, battled cancer, or lost a child say, "I would have never chosen this experience for my life, but neither would I trade the good things that have come into my life as a result of the pain I've experienced." Those "good things" that come out of the crucible of pain sometimes include the outpouring of concern from fellow Christians, deeper love for family members and friends, and a greater sense of the reality of God.

Joni Eareckson Tada, who has spent more than four decades as a quadriplegic as the result of a diving accident, is often quoted as saying she would rather be in a wheelchair with God than be able to walk without God. As a seventeen-year-old girl, would she willingly have chosen to hit her head as she dove into the Chesapeake Bay and suffer a lifetime of paralysis, even if she were able to see all of the positive benefits that would accrue in her life? No seventeen-year-old I know would make such a choice.

Fortunately, God does not solicit our input about the plans He has formulated for us. Just as most young children, if given the choice, would opt out of attending school, most of us would choose never to suffer any pain in our life. But like a child who spent all of his time on the playground instead of the classroom, we would be deprived of an invaluable education.

God uses pain—even pain that is inflicted by evil people with evil motives—for good in our lives. Or, as Joni says from the vantage point of a wheelchair, "God permits what He hates to achieve what He loves."[24]

GOD WILL ULTIMATELY DEFEAT EVIL AND END SUFFERING

The danger in writing a chapter like this one is that it can be misunderstood and misused. I am under no illusion that I have definitively answered the question of suffering and evil in the world at large or in your world in particular. Yet it seems there is an unrelenting desire in all of us to offer simplistic answers to unfathomable questions. Even those who should know better can't seem to help themselves. A few years ago a television evangelist made headlines by claiming an earthquake that had killed thousands was God's judgment against a nation that had made a pact with the devil hundreds of years earlier.

A television interviewer asked me what I thought about the evangelist's pronouncement, and I reminded her of Jesus' warning in Luke 13. A tower near the pool of Siloam had fallen, killing eighteen people. Random accidents like this pose no philosophical problem for unbelievers. High winds, faulty construction, deteriorating bricks, or a deliberate act of terrorism could explain why the tower fell. Stuff happens.

However, those who believe in an all-powerful deity who either caused or allowed this disaster to occur feel the need to answer the "why" question in a way that allows them to sleep better at night. They don't want to believe that their future well-being depends upon the whims of a capricious God who goes around toppling towers on innocent bystanders.

Knowing people's penchant to grab easy answers to complex problems, Jesus anticipated His listeners' answer to the "why" question and beat them to the punch:

Or do you suppose that those eighteen on whom the tower in Siloam fell and killed them were worse culprits than all the men who live in Jerusalem? I tell you, no. (Luke 13:4–5)

We naturally want to believe that bad things happen to people because those people are bad—or at least a little worse than we are. But Jesus said towers fall on both the righteous and the unrighteous. The earthquake I mentioned earlier destroyed the lives of both occult worshippers *and* Christian missionaries. That is why it is foolish and futile to try to offer definitive answers to the "why" question to anyone who is buckling under the weight of unrelenting pain.

However, we can offer comforting insights: God is in control, God is loving, and God can use evil for our ultimate good. And we can also say without hesitation that God will ultimately defeat evil and end our suffering. Just because God has not eliminated evil and suffering in the world yet does not mean He is not going to do so in the future.

Why doesn't God stamp out all the suffering in the world right now? For God to end all of the suffering in the world He would have to put an end to the cause of that suffering: rebellion against God (or, as the Bible calls it, "sin"). For God to end all rebellion against Himself means He would have to end history as we know it with a final and eternal judgment of the righteous and the unrighteous. The moment that final judgment occurs, all opportunity for repentance and salvation will be gone. People's destinies will be fixed for all eternity. The apostle Peter offers this insight about why God has not yet ended suffering, sin, and, therefore, the world as we know it:

> The Lord is not slow about His promise, as some count slowness, but is patient toward you, not wishing for any to perish but for all to come to repentance. But the day of the Lord *will* come like a thief, in which the heavens *will* pass away with a roar and the elements *will* be destroyed with intense heat, and the earth and its works *will* be burned up. (2 Peter 3:9–10)

Make no mistake about it: God is going to defeat evil and end suffering. Mercy, not apathy or impotence, is God's only reason for delaying the elimination of evil. Anytime you begin to doubt the certainty of evil's ultimate defeat, look back at the cross. The death of Jesus Christ represents the moment in time when God assured all of His creation that He was not about to allow sin and its devastating consequences to be the final word in human history. When Jesus cried out, "It is finished" (literally, "paid in full") in John 19:30, the countdown clock begin ticking away the seconds until God reclaims and re-creates His creation. After all, the best way to defeat evil is to create a new world where evil no longer exists.

In his book *Know Doubt*, John Ortberg invites readers to imagine you are a parent with a five-year-old who needs an operation. The doctor assures you that the operation is important but without any risk and will result in your child's healing. You are thrilled to know that such an operation is possible, but your child is scared to death. You do everything you can to assure her that everything will be fine, but she cannot comprehend that. Out of sensitivity to her feelings you mask your elation over the knowledge that your child will be just fine. While you genuinely empathize with her fear, you have a hard time not smiling, knowing that everything is going to work out in the end. In fact, occasionally you have to leave the hospital room because you feel the need to laugh because you already know the end of the story. Ortberg writes:

> What if the human condition is something like this. . . . What if all things are going to be well? What if Jesus knew this? Really knew? Then everything would have looked different to him. God would be the parent, and we would be the five-year-old in the sickroom. And God would have to accommodate himself to us; he would have to knit his brow and nod his head and take our fear seriously. But every once in a while God would have to excuse himself just to go outside and laugh.[25]

The fact that evil and suffering will ultimately be defeated in no way minimizes the intensity of the pain we feel now . . . and God understands that. Author Philip Yancey's father was a devout Christian and gifted Bible teacher. Yet in the final years of his life he suffered from a debilitating nerve disease that left him confined to a bed. He watched his adult daughter suffer the effects of a severe form of diabetes. He experienced crushing financial pressure. At the height of his personal crisis he sent a letter to his family members confessing that he was starting to question many of the things he once believed and taught others. But there were three truths about which Yancey remained absolutely certain:

> Life is difficult.
> God is merciful.
> Heaven is for sure.[26]

Good words to remember when passing through the tunnel of suffering.

CHAPTER FIVE

HOW CAN I KNOW I'M GOING TO HEAVEN WHEN I DIE?

The British playwright David Lodge was watching one of his plays in England on the evening of November 22, 1963. The audience laughed as the main character in the play came to a job interview holding a transistor radio next to his ear, showing his obvious indifference toward the interviewer. The character set down the radio and allowed it to play as background noise as the characters continued their dialogue. However, a newscaster interrupted the actual broadcast with a bulletin: "Today, the American president John F. Kennedy was assassinated. . . ." The audience gasped at the announcement. The actor tried to turn the radio off, but it was too late. The suspension of disbelief that allows a theater audience to forget the outside world for several hours as they enter a fantasy created by the writer had been pierced by the reality of death.[1]

In his book *The Denial of Death*, Ernest Becker writes that "the idea of death, the fear of it, haunts the human animal like nothing else."[2] Perhaps that is why we do everything we can to avoid the inevitability of death. Work, recreational pursuits, and relationships are welcomed diversions from the knowledge we all instinctively possess that every passing second moves us closer to the date of our demise.

Although death is all around us, we try to ignore it and go on. Author Saul Bellow says the living are like birds flying over the surface of the water. One bird may plunge into the water and never surface again, but the rest of the birds keep flying. Every day nearly five thousand Americans die, but we cannot afford to pause and consider our own mortality for long. The thought is too terrifying.

But occasionally death strikes so close to home that it pierces the suspension of disbelief we have created for ourselves. Consider the story of the Old Testament patriarch Job. Work, wealth, and the worship of God were integral parts of Job's world that kept him from thinking too much about his mortality. However, a freak storm that claimed the lives of all of his ten children shattered Job's self-created bubble and motivated him to cry out to God with the bottom-line question of human existence: "If a man dies, will he live again?" (Job 14:14). When you think about it, every other question in life pales in significance to this one.

- If my mate dies, will he live again?
- If my child dies, will I see her again?
- When I shut my eyes for the last time here on earth, will I slip into an eternity of nothingness or is there some other existence beyond the grave?

Every other question we have examined in this book is important, but none is as far-reaching as whether or not there is any existence beyond death. If this life is all that there is, then we should discard the claims of Christianity and find a new paradigm for living. The "eat, drink, and be merry for tomorrow we die" philosophy makes perfect sense if we place a period after the word "die." However, if our life on earth is only a brief prologue to an eternal existence that is determined by our beliefs and behavior on this side of the grave, then we would be wise to adopt a different philosophy for living in the here and now.

LIFE AFTER LIFE?

Is there any evidence for a positive response to Job's question? Is there life after life and death? An easy way to bring this chapter to a quick conclusion would be to say, "See the Bible." After all, since we have already established—at least in some readers' minds—that the Bible is God's Word to us and can be trusted to tell the truth, it would be easy to quote numerous passages in both the Old and New Testaments as prima facie evidence for a post-death existence. But given the importance of this question, we naturally wonder, "Is there any additional evidence *beyond* the Bible for life after life?"

I believe that there are four extrabiblical evidences for the existence of life beyond the grave. Admittedly, some are stronger than others and none is conclusive on its own, much like the circumstantial evidence collected at a crime scene. Individual pieces of evidence by themselves may not be enough to answer the "Who done it?" question, but when considered collectively they may point in a definite direction. Similarly, these four clues point in the direction of an existence that transcends our life on earth.

Near-Death Experiences

You have probably read or heard about the experiences of people who were close to death and in some cases met the qualifications of being declared clinically dead. While in this near-death or clinically dead state, some of these individuals report being transported to another world, meeting loved ones who have already died, or possessing an awareness of what was happening around them while unconscious. Since the publication of Raymond Moody's *Life after Life* in 1975, the number of people reporting near-death experiences (NDEs) has increased substantially. One poll conducted more than thirty years ago revealed that eight million Americans claimed to have had an NDE.[3]

Recent bestselling books such as Todd Burpo's *Heaven Is for Real*[4] and Don Piper's *90 Minutes in Heaven*[5] have captivated Christian readers with accounts of Christians whose near-death experiences transported them into the kind of heaven described in the Bible. *Heaven Is for Real* relates the experience of four-year-old Colton Burpo, who had an NDE during emergency surgery and later reported to his family about his three-minute journey to heaven. While there, Colton claims that he saw his sister who had died in his mother's womb (and about whom his parents had never told him), his great-grandfather, Jesus, and John the Baptist. Colton describes the occupants of heaven as possessing wings and halos, with an appearance that more closely resembles artistic depictions rather than biblical descriptions of those in the next world.

Although books like these have brought comfort and hope to millions of people, I am somewhat skeptical of them and NDEs in general for several reasons. First, the term "near-death experience" is somewhat akin to a "near-pregnant experience." Either you are, or you aren't. Nearly dead is not dead! For those of us who accept the veracity of the Bible we cannot ignore Hebrews 9:27: "It is appointed for men to die *once* and after this comes judgment." Although Jesus brought Lazarus to life after he had died, Lazarus had nothing to say about what happened to him while he was dead. The apostle Paul relates an account in 2 Corinthians 12 of being transported to heaven while either dead or unconscious—he couldn't say for sure. But the apostle was commanded not to describe what he saw (vv. 1–4). Neither of these men died, took a brief tour of heaven, and came back to write a best-selling book about the experience.

Also, these books unintentionally fuel the belief that the Bible is not sufficient to tell us everything we need to know about life after death. Many people have told me that these bestsellers gave them comfort about loved ones who had died. Yet isn't that what the Bible is supposed to do? If God thought we needed more information about what happens to us when we die, He could have removed the "news embargo" from Lazarus and the apostle Paul and allowed them to tell about their experiences in the next world. But He didn't.

Neither Burpo's nor Piper's book substantially contradicts the biblical revelation about the afterlife, and both books may be based on actual experiences. While I have no reason to doubt the sincerity of either author, I do think that near-death experiences are the weakest evidence for the reality of life after death. But given the number of these experiences, they should not be completely dismissed. At the very least, these near-death experiences suggest that consciousness can survive the cessation of heart and brain activity for some undetermined period of time, suggesting that there is some kind of existence that transcends physical life.

The Transcendence of the Mind

Professor Peter Kreeft claims that every time he deliberately moves his arm, he is proving the existence of a reality that transcends the material world. Beyond his muscles, nervous system, and brain there is a conscious will that controls the activities of his material body. This invisible reality is impossible to measure (how many centimeters wide is a person's will?) but is nevertheless observable every day of our lives. Kreeft argues that since our mind (also sometimes described as our "will" or "soul") is not part of the material world, there is no reason to assume that it ceases to exist when our physical body dies. Professor Kreeft writes, "The argument is so simple and evident that one wonders who the real primitive is: the savage who understands it or the sophisticated modern materialist who cannot understand the difference between the mind and the brain."[6]

Dirty Jokes and Death

C. S. Lewis once observed that almost all dirty jokes have to do with two natural acts: reproduction and excretion. Every other animal in the created world performs these functions routinely without hiding, blushing, or giggling about them. The fact that human beings are so focused on these natural behaviors is evidence of the dissonance that exists in every person between his spirit and his natural body.

That dissonance is also manifested in our discomfort with death. Even though death is a part of everything in the natural world from grass to grasshoppers, we human beings have a difficult time accepting the fact that we and everyone we care about will die. Author Philip Yancey says our reluctance to accept the physical consequences of death is seen in our rituals surrounding death: making up and dressing the corpses of our loved ones in their finest clothes and placing them in expensive caskets.

Yet nothing we do can prevent the inevitable decay of the physical body. Why are we so resistant to an experience that is so universal? Perhaps our innate rebellion against death is best explained by Solomon's claim that God has "set eternity" in our hearts (Ecclesiastes 3:11). We refuse to accept the finality of death because we instinctively know that death is not the end of human experience, and therefore we rebel against anything that suggests otherwise.

You probably have never thought of dirty jokes and death as evidence of life after death. Admittedly, they don't offer conclusive proof on their own but are important pieces of evidence to consider. Yancey writes, "It is natural that we blush at excretion and rear back from death—natural, that is, if you accept a biblical view of humanity. Excretion and death seem odd because they are odd. In all earth there are no exact parallels of spirit and immortality trapped in matter. The unnaturalness and discomfiture we feel may be our most accurate human sensations, reminding us we are not quite 'at home' here."[7]

The Empty Tomb

Using Jesus' resurrection as evidence for existence beyond death may sound as if I have just resorted to circular reasoning: using the Bible to prove the veracity of the Bible. After all, I promised at the beginning of this section to look at evidence outside of the Bible for the reality of an afterlife. However, the empty tomb of Jesus represents extrabiblical evidence for life after death. Let me explain.

Recently I took a group of our church members to Israel, and on the last day of our trip we visited the site that many people believe was the tomb of Jesus Christ. Our group entered that small opening in the side of a cliff two at a time. When one of our members emerged he yelled out to those of us still waiting to enter, "He's *still* not there!" Now, admittedly, it is altogether possible that we were not in the actual spot where Christ was buried, which would explain why we saw no physical remains of Jesus.

That is why I'm using the term "empty tomb" as a synonym for "the absence of a body." The fact that Jesus' body has not been discovered in the more than two thousand years after His death is strong evidence for the reality of life after death—especially when you consider the following facts that can be verified outside of the Bible:

1. Jesus is accepted almost universally as a historical figure.
2. His followers have claimed for more than two thousand years that He was miraculously raised from the dead. They assert that His resurrection is the signal proof that He was the Son of God.
3. His detractors, beginning with the Roman and Jewish authorities who called for His execution, have denied this claim and have continuously sought to extinguish the Christian movement since its inception.

Since the resurrection is central to the Christian faith, you would assume that the enemies of Christianity—beginning with those Jewish and Roman authorities who ordered His death—would have done everything they could to produce the body of Christ. Had Jesus' remains been discovered, Christianity would have been stillborn at its conception. Yet from the time of the claimed resurrection of Jesus until now, Christianity has exploded in numbers and influence across the globe—all because no body of Jesus has ever been discovered. But Christianity's critics insist that the resurrection is a fairy tale.

The Latin phrase *habeas corpus* means "you have the body." A "writ of habeas corpus" is a legal order requiring that a prisoner be produced and brought before a judge who can determine whether there is sufficient evidence to continue holding the prisoner captive. This order prevents the unlawful detention of prisoners. Many non-Christians today are being held captive by the belief that Christ's resurrection is a myth. They have embraced the common storyline about Jesus spun by the critics of Christianity that goes something like this:

> Jesus was a great teacher who lived an exemplary life and was unjustly martyred by religious and political zealots. However, another group of zealots attempted to seize power from the Roman/Jewish political establishment by creating the myth that Jesus was the Son of God and miraculously rose from the dead three days after His crucifixion. Unfortunately, this myth of Christ's resurrection continues to be perpetuated by power-hungry clergymen and the ignorant masses they have successfully duped.

I believe that it is time to order the critics of Christianity who continue to espouse the above version of Christ's life a "writ of habeas corpus" for Jesus Christ. If He has not risen from the dead, then show us His body! Surely after two thousand years of opportunity they could have produced the body of Jesus Christ if it had been left behind. Since they are incapable of producing the body of Jesus, it is time to set free the prisoners of unbelief.

The absence of Jesus' body is a historically verifiable reality (no credible person has even claimed to have discovered it) with obvious ramifications in the question of after-death existence. If it can be demonstrated that at least one individual in history has lived beyond his death, then you have proved the existence of life after death.

Does the absence of Jesus' body prove the reality of an afterlife? No, not any more than near-death experiences, the transcendence of the mind, dirty jokes, and our aversion to death prove that there is life after death. However, when considered together, these clues seem to point to the same conclusion: physical death does not mark the end of our existence.

WHAT OTHER RELIGIONS SAY ABOUT THE AFTERLIFE

The various major world religions all propose some kind of existence beyond physical death. While several of these religions share similar views of the nature of the afterlife, most stand in stark contrast to one another.

Hinduism

Hindus believe that we are caught in an endless cycle of birth, death, and rebirth in this illusory world. The ultimate goal of Hinduism is salvation from this endless cycle and either an eternal resting place with God or the dissolution of individual personality into the abyss of Brahman.

Buddhism

Since life is filled with suffering and dissatisfaction, the key to salvation is to put an end to our natural craving for pleasure, wealth, and power by following the Noble Eightfold Path. The ultimate goal of Buddhism is reaching the state of being known as "nirvana," which means "blowing out"—like the extinguishing of a candle. True happiness only occurs when we have extinguished our cravings in life that lead to dissatisfaction. Nirvana represents an eternal state of enlightenment that is void of craving and, therefore, dissatisfaction.

Mormonism

The Church of Jesus Christ of Latter-day Saints teaches that there are three heavens. The highest heaven, known as the Celestial Kingdom, is reserved for the most faithful Mormons. It is the only one of the three heavens in which people can live forever with their earthly families. The next heaven is the Terrestrial Kingdom and is inhabited by those who rejected the gospel on earth but accepted it after death. Also living there will be those Mormons and non-Mormons who did not obey God's laws to the best of their abilities.

The lowest heaven, called the Telestial Kingdom, is reserved for those who reject the gospel in this life, as well as the chance to repent in the next life. Unrepentant murderers and adulterers will reside here. Nevertheless, Mormons believe this kingdom is still so splendid that people in this life would be willing to commit suicide in order to reside there. Mormons do believe in a type of hell, but it is reserved for a very small fraction of humanity known as the "sons of perdition." The vast majority of humanity will exist in one of the three heavens.

Islam

The religion of Islam shares similarities with Christianity regarding the nature of the afterlife but is vastly different in its teaching about the way to ensure one's well-being in the next life. Islam claims that life on earth is transitory and preparatory for eternity. Muhammad, the founder of Islam, taught that there will be a future resurrection of both the righteous and the unrighteous for the Last Judgment, resulting in bliss for the former and torment for the latter.

Heaven is viewed as an extension of the Garden of Eden, whose splendor is beyond human comprehension. Hell is pictured as a place of punishment, complete with the fire and brimstone described in the Bible. One of the major differences between the Islamic and Christian view of the afterlife is that Islam denies that heaven and hell are eternal states, since only Allah is infinite.

Judaism

Judaism embraces the belief that there is a future resurrection, judgment by God, and final assignment to one of two eternal states. According to the prophet Daniel, "Many of those who sleep in the dust of the ground will awake, these to everlasting life, but the others to disgrace and everlasting contempt" (Daniel 12:2). Although traditional Judaism teaches an existence beyond death, the focus of Judaism has been on living righteously in this life in order to merit whatever rewards God may dispense in the next life.

While it is theoretically possible that all views of the afterlife (including the Christian view) are wrong, it is impossible that they can all be correct, given the substantive differences between these various religions. Obviously, it is impossible to prove or disprove any of these theories of life after death independent of the religious texts or teachings on which they are based. Thus, the person who wants to ensure his eternal well-being must decide on which religion he is willing to entrust his eternal destiny.

In chapter 3 I explained how you can know that Christianity is the most trustworthy religion to choose. If you decide to embrace Christianity, then it only makes sense to embrace *all* of Christianity, including its teachings about the afterlife. Viewing religion as a spiritual buffet in which you pick and choose beliefs from each faith that are most palatable to you makes no sense, especially if some of those beliefs are toxic and can lead to spiritual death. So what does Christianity teach about the nature of life beyond death?

THE INEVITABILITY OF DEATH

The Bible affirms what is readily observable to all of us: no one gets out of this world alive. As one wag said, "The statistics on death are very impressive: one out of every one dies." Admittedly, it seems unjust that everyone would experience the same fate regardless of his conduct here on earth. Solomon wrestled with the inequity of the universality of death:

It is the same for all. There is one fate for the righteous and for the wicked; for the good, for the clean, and for the unclean; for the man who offers a sacrifice and for the one who does not sacrifice. As the good man is, so is the sinner; as the swearer is, so is the one who is the one who is afraid to swear. This is an evil in all that is done under the sun. (Ecclesiastes 9:2–3)

Two men who lived two very different kinds of lives both died on June 25, 2009. One man was Michael Jackson—perhaps you've heard of him. Tens of millions of people around the globe watched the memorial service of this entertainer who earned hundreds of millions of dollars during his relatively brief career.

Also on that day Edwin Clayton died. Although most people have never heard of him, Clayton served for thirty-four years as the pastor of Tomahawk Baptist Church in Midlothian, Virginia. There were no crowds in the street at his funeral or around-the-clock media retrospectives about his life and career.

One man lived for himself and the other lived for God. One had fame and riches, while the other lived in obscurity. One man's life was marked by scandal, while the other man's life was a model of faithfulness. Yet both men died. Where is the fairness in that?

Solomon knew the answer. Although there is one fate for all human beings, there are two very different destinies beyond death for the righteous and unrighteous. Solomon believed that there was a judgment by God that awaited every person beyond death: "'God will judge both the righteous man and the wicked man,' for a time for every matter and for every deed is there" (Ecclesiastes 3:17).

Jesus Christ also affirmed that there are two very different roads in this life that lead to two distinct destinies in the next life:

Enter through the narrow gate; for the gate is wide and the way is broad that leads to destruction, and there are many who enter through it. For the gate is small and the way is narrow that leads to life, and there are few who find it. (Matthew 7:13–14)

The reality of two possible destinies for us after we die is most clearly taught by Jesus in His story about a rich man and a poor man named Lazarus. These two men could not have experienced more disparate lives. The wealthy man lived a luxurious existence, while Lazarus had to subsist on the crumbs that fell from the rich man's table. Yet in spite of these inequities while on earth, both men experienced the same fate: death. But Jesus' story doesn't stop at the cemetery:

Now the poor man died and was carried away by the angels to Abraham's bosom; and the rich man also died and was buried. In Hades he lifted up his eyes, being in torment. (Luke 16:22–23)

These two men, who lived two very different existences, experienced two radically different destinies. What are these two possible eternal destinies that await us?

WHAT JESUS SAID ABOUT HELL

Hell is one possible destination for those who die. Jesus consistently warned about the reality of hell. Of the 1,850 verses in the New Testament that record Jesus' words, 13 percent of them deal with the subject of eternal judgment and hell. In fact, Jesus spoke more frequently about hell than He did about heaven. Unless you are going to pick and choose which of Jesus' words to believe or disbelieve, you must draw some conclusion about Jesus' teaching about hell. It is intellectually dishonest to say, "I believe Jesus was a great moral teacher, or perhaps even the Son of God, but I refuse to believe what He said about hell." His extensive teaching on hell does not allow that option.

If Jesus were wrong about His belief in the existence of a place of eternal torment for the wicked, then His erroneous teaching could only be explained in one of two ways. If Jesus were sincerely mistaken about hell—He actually believed in a place that did not exist—then He could not have been the Son of God since He did not know what destiny awaited unbelievers.

However, if Jesus willingly misled His followers about hell—if He taught about a place that He knew did not exist—then He is guilty of deception and is morally disqualified to be the Messiah. If you believe that Jesus is the Son of God and therefore incapable of speaking untruth due to a lack of knowledge or integrity, then you cannot ignore what He says about hell. What did Jesus believe and teach about hell?

Hell Is an Actual Location

The New Testament uses three different words that are translated "hell" in most English versions of the Bible. The word *tartaros* is used in 2 Peter 2:4 to describe the place where a select group of wicked angels are dispatched because of a sin described in Jude 6.

The most commonly used word for hell is "Gehenna," which describes the eternal destiny of unbelievers. Gehenna referred to the Valley of Hinnom located south of Jerusalem. The Israelites living under the reigns of the wicked kings Ahaz and Manasseh would offer their children as burnt sacrifices in this valley. Later, the valley was used as a garbage dump where both the refuse of the city and the bodies of executed criminals were burned day and night. One can hardly imagine a more repulsive place in which to spend an hour, much less eternity, than the Valley of Hinnom. Yet, eleven times Jesus used this location as a description of the eternal destination of the unrighteous.

The third word that is used for hell is "Hades." Jesus chose this word to describe the temporary residing place for the unrighteous as they await their final judgment that will send them to Gehenna (referred to in Revelation 20:14 as "the lake of fire"). Jesus used this term in Luke 16:23, describing the rich man who died as being in "Hades." Although Hades is a temporary location for unbelievers, it is characterized as a place of intense suffering. Jesus described the rich man in Hades as "being in torment" and crying out for relief from his physical pain (Luke 16:23–24). After the final judgment of all unbelievers at the end of time, known as the Great White Throne Judgment, the apostle John foresees the occupants of Hades being dispatched into the lake of fire (or, as Jesus described it, "Gehenna") for all eternity:

> Then death and Hades were thrown into the lake of fire. This is the second death, the lake of fire. (Revelation 20:14)

It is increasingly popular to claim that hell is simply a state of mind more than an actual location. Some writers, like former pastor Rob Bell, theorize that everyone goes to the same realm when they die: for some this realm is "heaven" and for others it is "hell," depending on a person's spiritual orientation in this life. However, Jesus Christ clearly taught that there are two different destinations for the righteous and the unrighteous:

> These will go away into eternal punishment, but the righteous into eternal life. (Matthew 25:46)

If you believe that heaven is an actual location and not a state of mind (and there is plenty of reason to believe that, as we will see in the next section), then you must also accept the spatial reality of hell. Why? It would have been illogical for Jesus to have said unbelievers "go away" into a state of mind, while the righteous go to an actual location. Jesus believed that both the unrighteous and the righteous will spend eternity in a place, not a state of mind.

Hell Is a Place of Indescribable and Eternal Torment

Jesus described the rich man who died as experiencing unspeakable physical pain:

> And he [the rich man] cried out and said, "Father Abraham, have mercy on me, and send Lazarus so that he may dip the tip of his finger in water and cool off my tongue, for I am in agony in this flame." (Luke 16:24)

In Mark 9:48 Jesus also used the imagery of fire to describe the horror of hell: "where THEIR WORM DOES NOT DIE, AND THE FIRE IS NOT QUENCHED." So terrible is the suffering in hell that its occupants will engage in a continual "weeping and gnashing of teeth" (Matthew 22:13).

In an attempt to "turn down the temperature" of hell, some have speculated that the fire Jesus describes in these passages should not be taken literally but instead be understood as a symbol of God's purifying judgment. While it is true that Jesus frequently employed metaphors to communicate spiritual truth, one cannot find any relief from the horrors of hell if He is doing so in this passage. If Jesus is using fire metaphorically, then He is saying that the reality of hell is so painful that it defies description. The only way to approximate the suffering of hell is to imagine the burning of one's flesh for eternity.

Some Christians who have difficulty believing that God would torment unbelievers forever have embraced annihilationism. Instead of burning eternally, this theory postulates that unbelievers are cast into the lake of fire, where they are destroyed. While this view is more palatable for those who cannot imagine a loving God punishing unbelievers forever, annihilationism finds no support from the Bible. Jesus said that unbelievers will experience "eternal punishment" just as believers will experience "eternal life" (Matthew 25:46). If you shorten the duration of "eternal punishment" by any amount of time, you must also equally diminish the duration of "eternal life." One minute less in hell for unbelievers means one minute less in heaven for believers.

Furthermore, the Bible indicates that the lake of fire, which is the eternal destination of unbelievers, does not destroy its occupants. In Revelation 19:20 both the beast (commonly known as the Antichrist) and the false prophet are cast into the lake of fire when Jesus Christ returns to earth. One thousand years after this event, prior to the judgment of all unbelievers (known as the Great White Throne Judgment), the apostle John sees Satan being cast into this same lake of fire:

> The devil who deceived them was thrown into the lake of fire and brimstone where the beast and the false prophet are also; and they will be tormented day and night forever and ever. (Revelation 20:10)

Notice John does not say "where the beast and false prophet *were*" but "where the beast and the false prophet *are*." If the lake of fire instantly destroyed those who are sent there, then "were" would have been the appropriate word. However, the lake of fire is a place of eternal punishment, not immediate destruction. After one thousand years in the lake of fire, the beast and false prophet "are" still alive.

Tragically, the lake of fire will be populated by more than Satan, the beast, and false prophet. All of humanity from the beginning of time who have rejected Christ's offer of forgiveness will experience eternal torment:

> Then death and Hades were thrown into the lake of fire. This is the second death, the lake of fire. And if anyone's name was not found written in the book of life, he was thrown into the lake of fire. (Revelation 20:14–15)

Hell Will Contain the Majority of Humanity

Many polls reveal that the majority of Americans believe in the existence of hell, but only a small percentage of people believe *they* will go there. Most people see the moral rationale for a place of punishment for truly evil people like Adolph Hitler, Charles Manson, and Osama bin Laden. But it is unthinkable to many people that all those who have not trusted in Jesus for forgiveness would be sentenced to hell.

What about the billions of people around the globe who are sincere followers of other religions or have simply found a way to live moral lives without any religion? Since only a minority of the world's population has embraced Christ's message, are we prepared to say that the majority of the world's population will spend eternity being tormented by God simply because they have not chosen to embrace Christianity? Former pastor Rob Bell vehemently denies the implication that the majority of humanity will spend eternity in hell:

> A staggering number of people have been taught that a select few Christians will spend forever in a peaceful, joyous place called heaven while the rest of humanity will spend forever in torment and punishment in hell with no chance for anything better. It's been clearly communicated to many that this belief is a central truth of the Christian faith and to reject it is, in essence to reject Jesus. This is misguided, toxic, and ultimately subverts the contagious spread of Jesus' message of love, peace, and forgiveness and joy that our world desperately needs to hear.[8]

Yet in spite of the protests of Bell and others, Jesus clearly taught that only a small percentage of humanity will find the way to eternal life, meaning that the majority of mankind will occupy hell:

> Enter through the narrow gate; for the gate is wide and the way is broad that leads to destruction, and there are many who enter

through it. For the gate is small and the way is narrow that leads to life, and there are few who find it. (Matthew 7:13–14)

Furthermore, Jesus asserted that hell is not just populated by mass murderers, rapists, and drug dealers. Hell will also be occupied by sincere, religious people who perform good works in the name of Jesus Christ. Jesus warned about the surprise that awaits many people at the final judgment:

Not everyone who says to Me, "Lord, Lord," will enter the kingdom of heaven, but he who does the will of My father who is in heaven will enter. Many will say to Me on that day, "Lord, Lord, did we not prophesy in Your name, and in Your name cast out demons, and in Your name perform many miracles?" And then I will declare to them, "I never knew you; DEPART FROM ME, YOU WHO PRACTICE LAWLESSNESS." (Matthew 7:21–23)

Why do so many of us struggle with Jesus' declaration that the majority of humanity (including good, religious people) will be sent to hell? First, we have a low view of God. We assume that God should be just as tolerant of sin in other people as we are. However, the reason we can accept sin in others and in ourselves is not because we are so much like God, but because we are so *unlike* God. "You thought that I was just like you," God reminded the Israelites in Psalm 50:21. However, God is not like us but instead is One whose "eyes are too pure to approve evil" and who cannot "look on wickedness with favor" (Habakkuk 1:13).

Coupled with our low view of God, most of us embrace a high view of ourselves that causes us to doubt that eternal torment is a just punishment for the majority of humanity—or for us. Our inflated view of our own goodness explains why so few Americans believe they deserve to go to hell. The standard we utilize to evaluate our relative goodness is usually people we deem to be worse than we are (adulterers and murderers rather than priests and nuns). Using that flawed measurement we arrive at the equally flawed conclusion that we are fairly decent people and do not deserve to be consigned to the flames of hell for eternity.

However, the standard God uses to evaluate our goodness is not other people, but God's own perfection. Of course, by that standard we all fall short. For example, the geographical distance between the North and South Pole is great, but is also negligible compared to the distance between the North Pole and the farthest star in the universe. Similarly, the moral difference between an Adolph Hitler and you or me may seem substantial, but it is minimal compared to the difference between us and a perfect God. It is that great gulf between God's righteousness and ours that motivated Paul to write, "For all have sinned and fall short of the glory of God" (Romans 3:23). Unbelievers will spend eternity in hell, not because they are not good but because they are not good *enough*.

Hell Is a Forever Destination

Some people have theorized that those people who find themselves in hell (whatever that may be) don't necessarily have to remain in hell. For example, Rob Bell theorizes that after spending a brief time in hell (whatever that may be) even unbelievers will have a change of heart, repent, and be ushered into heaven (whatever that may be):

> At the heart of this perspective is the belief that, given enough time, everybody will turn to God and find themselves in the joy and peace of God's presence. The love of God will melt every hard heart, even the most "depraved sinners" will eventually give up their resistance and turn to God.[9]

What would lead Bell to think that people in hell could change their minds and choose to follow God? In an interview with CNN Bell said, "With this world right now we are free to choose. So when you die, I would assume you can continue to make those types of choices."[10]

Basing one's beliefs about eternity on assumptions (such as the assumption that repentance is possible after we die) can be lethal, especially when those assumptions are in direct contradiction with Jesus Christ's teachings. In the story of the rich man and Lazarus, Jesus describes the wealthy occupant of hell as having a change of heart, evidenced by his concern for the eternal destiny of his brothers who are still alive. The wealthy occupant of hell begs Abraham for physical relief from his torment. Then he pleads with Abraham to send Lazarus to warn his siblings about the awful fate that awaits those who die apart from God. Abraham explains why he cannot fulfill either request:

> And besides all this, between us and you there is a great chasm fixed, so that those who wish to come over from here to you may not be able, and that *none may cross over from there to us*. (Luke 16:26)

Jesus declared that the great gulf between hell and heaven is "fixed," meaning that no one can ever travel from hell to heaven or from heaven to hell. But what if an occupant of hell believes in Jesus Christ and accepts His forgiveness? It is too late, Jesus taught. In hell, everyone is a believer.

Fortunately, there is an alternative to this terrible place about which Jesus warned.

WHAT JESUS SAID ABOUT HEAVEN

Jesus, along with the writers of the New Testament, often talked about a place we commonly refer to as "heaven." Admittedly, the details of heaven are incomplete—probably for good reason. If we actually knew what awaited us in heaven, Christians might engage in mass suicides to reach our eternal destination more quickly. At the very least, a full understanding of our existence after death might make it difficult to concentrate on the very real responsibilities God has given us here on earth, much like a child trying to eat his meat and vegetables at dinner while looking at an ice cream sundae that has been set before him.

However, the New Testament provides us with enough of a taste of heaven to whet our appetites for this future possibility. The Bible reveals five important realities about heaven.

Heaven Is an Actual Location

Any attempt to relegate either hell or heaven to a state of mind rather than an actual location is contrary to the teaching of Jesus Christ and the revelation of the New Testament. If you have ever attended a Christian funeral you have probably heard the minister quote one of the most familiar promises from Jesus about the certainty of heaven:

> Do not let your heart be troubled; believe in God, believe also in Me. In My father's house are many dwelling *places*; if it were not so, I would have told you; for I go to prepare a *place* for you. And if I go and prepare a *place* for you, I will come again and receive you to Myself, that where I am, there you may be also. (John 14:1–3)

Jesus uses the word "place" or "places" three times in these three verses to describe heaven. The word translated "place" is the Greek word *topos*, which was often used to describe a geographical destination. Furthermore, Jesus described this "place" as containing many "dwelling places" where His followers would live, denoting an actual location rather than a state of mind. Assume for a moment that Jesus wanted to communicate to us that heaven was an actual geographic destination rather than a state of mind. Could He have chosen any more precise language than that which He used here?

Additionally, consider Luke's account of Jesus' ascension into heaven forty days after His resurrection from the dead:

And after He had said these things, He was lifted up while they were looking on, and a cloud received Him out of their sight. And as they were gazing intently into the sky while He was going, behold, two men in white clothing stood beside them. They also said, "Men of Galilee, why do you stand looking into the sky? This Jesus, who has been taken up from you into heaven, will come in just the same way as you have watched Him go into heaven." (Acts 1:9–11)

As I stood on the Mount of Olives where this event occurred, I tried to imagine what an astonishing sight this must have been for all who witnessed it. The most natural question from the spectators would have been, "Where did Jesus go?" The angels told the assembled crowd that Jesus had gone "into heaven" and that one day He would return from heaven "in just the same way" in which He had departed. Now think about it. Did Jesus ascend from this very real earth into a state of mind? No, He simply changed locations from an earthly place to a heavenly place. And one day, Jesus will return from a heavenly location (not a state of mind) to this very real earth.

Heaven Is Both an Immediate and Ultimate Destination

We saw in the previous section that the word "hell" is used in the Bible to describe both the immediate destination of unbelievers (Hades) and the ultimate place of eternal torment (Gehenna or the lake of fire). Similarly, "heaven" is a generic term that is used to describe both the immediate and ultimate destination of Christians who die.

Jesus said that when Lazarus died, he "was carried away by the angels to Abraham's bosom" (Luke 16:22). The strong inference was that Lazarus experienced immediate relief after his difficult life in contrast to the rich man who experienced immediate torment in Hades. Just as the rich man was conscious of his pain, it can be assumed that Lazarus was also conscious of his new environment.

Jesus also assured the penitent thief on the cross that upon his death he would immediately begin to experience the joy of being in Christ's presence: "Today you shall be with Me in Paradise" (Luke 23:43). The apostle Paul comforted the Corinthian Christians with the assurance that for a believer to be "absent from the body" is "to be at home with the Lord" (2 Corinthians 5:8). Admittedly, the Bible does not reveal a great deal about this temporary destination for believers when they die other than it is an immediate destination, is much more desirable than Hades, and is the same location where Jesus Christ is.

However, when people use the term "heaven" they are most often thinking of the eternal destination of believers. Unlike "Abraham's bosom" or "Paradise," where Christians go immediately when they die, heaven is a future location that is still under construction. Jesus told His disciples that He was going back to heaven "to prepare a place" (John 14:2), indicating that this place had not yet been created. In Revelation 21, John describes "a new heaven and a new earth" and a "new Jerusalem, coming down out of heaven from God" only after "the first heaven and the first earth passed away" (vv. 1–2). The New Testament offers more details—though far from complete—about this eternal destination for Christians than it provides about the temporary location for Christians when they die.

Heaven Will Be Primarily a Re-Created Earth

One of the greatest misconceptions about heaven is that it is located in some distant galaxy far, far away or in some invisible fourth dimension that will be inhabited by the disembodied spirits of Christians. Nothing could be further from the truth. The Bible teaches that the ultimate dwelling place for Christians will be a re-created earth, not an ethereal and undefined location in outer space:

> Those who wait on the LORD, they shall inherit *the earth*.
> (Psalm 37:9 NKJV)

Blessed are the gentle, for they shall inherit *the earth*.
(Matthew 5:5)

But according to His promise we are looking for new heavens and a *new earth*, in which righteousness dwells. (2 Peter 3:13)

Remember that God's original plan was for people to dwell in and rule over the earth God had created specifically for them. Sin corrupted both mankind and the physical world in which they lived. But God had no intention of forfeiting the human race or the physical world to Satan. Instead, God sent Christ to redeem not only mankind, but the created world as well so that "the creation itself also will be set free from its slavery to corruption into the freedom of the glory of the children of God" (Romans 8:21).

God is just as intent on reclaiming a sinful earth as He is in rescuing sinful mankind from Satan's clutches. However, because both the earth and mankind have been infected with sin, God's reclamation of each requires a re-creation. The moment someone trusts in Christ for salvation, the process of re-creation begins with that person's spirit and continues until he ultimately receives a new physical body:

Therefore if anyone is in Christ, he is a new creature; the old things passed away; behold, new things have come. (2 Corinthians 5:17)

Similarly, the present heaven (referring to the earth's atmosphere and what we term "outer space," but not including the realm in which God exists) and the present earth will be destroyed (2 Peter 3:10–11), and God will create a new heaven and a new earth.

Then I saw a new heaven and a new earth; for the first heaven and the first earth passed away, and there is no longer any sea. And I saw the holy city, new Jerusalem, coming down out of heaven from God, made ready as a bride adorned for her husband. And I heard a loud voice from the throne, saying, "Behold, the tabernacle of God is among men, and He will dwell among them, and they shall be His people, and God Himself will be among them." (Revelation 21:1–3)

This new earth will be the center of God's re-created universe, and the focal point of this new earth will be an actual city called the "new Jerusalem." Later in Revelation 21, John gives a detailed description of the splendor of this city and also provides readers with a description of the city's size:

The city is laid out as a square, and its length is as great as the width; and he measured the city with the rod, fifteen hundred miles; its length and width and height are equal. (v. 16)

While some might be inclined to take these measurements symbolically, there really is no reason to do so since the number "fifteen hundred" is specific and is not used symbolically elsewhere in the Bible. If we take these measurements literally, a city this large would be the size of Ireland, Great Britain, France, Spain, Germany, Austria, Italy, Turkey, and half of Russia. Furthermore, although this city is the primary residing place for Christians, there is no reason to believe they will not be free to roam the rest of the earth or the universe.

My predecessor Dr. W. A. Criswell used to say that he found great comfort in the realization that earth, not some faraway heaven, would be his eternal residence. He often remarked, "I would not look forward to God's sending me out on some planet a hundred million miles away that I know nothing about. I like almost everything here on this earth. The only things I do not like are the tears and the separation of bereavement in the funerals and the graves and the heartache and despair they bring." But of course, those things will not be present in the newly created earth in which God "will wipe away every tear from their eyes; and there will no longer be any death; there will no longer be any mourning, or crying, or pain; the first things have passed away" (Revelation 21:4).

After the city known as the "new Jerusalem" descends from heaven to earth, the apostle John hears a voice proclaim, "Behold, the tabernacle of God is among men, and He will dwell among them" (Revelation 21:2–3). Author Randy Alcorn describes the eternal destination of Christians as "an unprecedented joining of heaven and earth, which have always been separate. The new earth is the cosmic center of the new heavens. It will be, literally, heaven on earth."[11]

Alcorn notes that the voice does not say that God will take us up to make our dwelling in His world. Instead, God will ultimately come down to make His dwelling in our world. Alcorn concludes with this wonderfully encouraging and enlightening insight:

> Going to heaven is not our going to a spiritual realm made by God for himself, a realm in which we don't really fit. Rather, it's God coming to enter a physical realm created by him for us, a realm in which we'll perfectly fit.[12]

Heaven Is a Continuum of Our Earthly Existence

Another common misconception about the eternal state—whether it be hell or heaven—is that there is no connection between our present life on earth and our eternity. However, the Bible describes our lives as a continuum that begins here on earth and extends beyond the grave.

For example, there is continuity between the present earth where we now reside and the new earth. Revelation 21–22 describes the beauty of the new earth with familiar imagery:

Then he showed me a river of the water of life, clear as crystal, coming from the throne of God and of the Lamb, in the middle of its street. And on either side of the river was the tree of life, bearing twelve kinds of fruit, yielding its fruit every month; and the leaves of the tree were for the healing of the nations. There will no longer be any curse. (Revelation 22:1–3)

"Tree of life," "fruit," and "no longer any curse" all remind the reader of God's original design for earth as represented in the Garden of Eden. John is describing the new earth as a kind of an Eden 2.0— retaining yet enhancing God's original design. The mountains, rivers, forests, and trees, and even animals that were part of God's original design will be present in the new earth. Think of the most beautiful places you have ever visited in the world (I'm picturing my favorite beach in Maui). The location you have in mind is only a pencil sketch of the splendor that God has in mind for Christians in the new earth.

There is also continuity between our earthly bodies and our eternal bodies. We will not spend eternity as disembodied spirits; instead, we will possess new bodies that are vastly superior, yet also similar, to our present bodies. Remember, God created you with a spirit, soul, and a body. Without all three of these components, you are not the person God created. There has never been a time in the past when you were just a spirit, and there will never be a time in the future when you exist without a body.

As I pastor I am frequently asked questions about eternal bodies:

- Will we all look the same in our new bodies?
- Will we recognize one another in heaven?
- Will we be able to eat in our new bodies?

If you wonder about what life will be like in your heavenly body, just look at the example of Jesus in His postresurrection appearances. For forty days after He was raised from the dead, Jesus lived on earth and made numerous appearances to people. One of the most famous of those postresurrection appearances is recorded in Luke 24 on the road to Emmaus. At first, the disciples did not recognize Him but were so enthralled by His words that they urged Him to have dinner with them:

> When He had reclined at the table with them, He took the bread and blessed it, and breaking it, He began giving it to them. Then their eyes were opened and they recognized Him; and He vanished from their sight. (Luke 24:30–31)

Later, Jesus appeared again to them for an even more involved interaction with His disciples:

> While they were telling these things, He Himself stood in their midst. But they were startled and frightened and thought that they were seeing a spirit. And He said to them, "Why are you troubled, and why do doubts arise in your hearts? See My hands and My feet, that it is I Myself; touch Me and see, for a spirit does not have flesh and bones as you see that I have." . . . While they still could not believe it because of their joy and amazement, He said to them, "Have you anything here to eat?" They gave Him a piece of broiled fish; and He took it and ate it before them. (Luke 24:36–39, 41–43)

Something about the way Jesus broke the bread caused His disciples to recognize the Lord. Perhaps He had been left-handed in His earthly body, and He retained that trait in His new body.

Jesus' new body also possessed some of the physical drives of His earthly body. While the disciples were still staring at Him, slack-jawed over what they were seeing, Jesus asked for something to eat! He not only desired food but demonstrated the ability to satisfy that desire by digesting the food before them, just as He had done countless times prior to His death.

Yet Jesus' new body was also different than His earthly one. For example, His physical appearance must have been somewhat different since it took His disciples some time to recognize Him. Also, Jesus' new body provided Him the ability to enter a room without the use of a door (which explains why the disciples were repeatedly startled and frightened when He appeared).

The reason Jesus' resurrection body is important to us is that He is described as "the firstborn from the dead" (Colossians 1:18). The word translated "firstborn" is the Greek word from which we get our English word *prototype*. Before an automobile company cranks up the assembly line to produce hundreds of thousands of copies of a new car, it first develops a prototype of that automobile after which all other copies are patterned. Jesus' resurrection body is a prototype of the body all of Christ's followers will receive one day. It will be similar but vastly superior to our earthly body, it will be recognizable by others, and it will be free from any remnant of sin's curse such as sickness or death.

The continuum between earth and heaven extends beyond the physical earth and our physical bodies to include the totality of our lives. The choices we make in this life have a shelf life that extends beyond our death and reverberates throughout eternity. For example, a person's decision to trust in Christ for the forgiveness of sins while he is still alive determines what happens to him after he dies:

> Jesus said to her, "I am the resurrection and the life; he who believes in Me will live even if he dies, and everyone who lives and believes in Me shall never die." (John 11:25–26)

The choices Christians make in this life will result in either the acquisition or forfeiture of eternal rewards in the next life:

Therefore we also have as our ambition, whether at home or absent, to be pleasing to Him. For we must all appear before the judgment seat of Christ, so that each one may be recompensed for his deeds in the body, according to what he has done, whether good or bad. (2 Corinthians 5:9–10)

Similarly, the decisions unbelievers make in this life also have eternal ramifications. Those who reject Christ's offer of forgiveness in this life will be judged according to their good works performed while they were alive:

And I saw the dead, the great and the small, standing before the throne, and books were opened; and another book was opened, which is the book of life; and the dead were judged from the things which were written in the books, according to their deeds. (Revelation 20:12)

At this final judgment, God will review the life record of everyone who has opted out of the "salvation by grace" plan and chosen the "salvation by works" plan. Unfortunately, no one's works will be good enough to merit entrance into heaven. The unbeliever's decision not to ask for Christ's forgiveness and have his name recorded in the book of life will result in eternal death:

And if anyone's name was not found written in the book of life, he was thrown into the lake of fire. (Revelation 20:15)

The unbeliever's actions on earth will be enough to condemn him to eternal death, while his inaction in receiving Christ's forgiveness will rob him of eternal life. In both cases there is a continuum between the unbeliever's life on earth that extends throughout eternity.

The most disturbing aspect of this continuum is that the unbeliever will be haunted for all eternity by the regret of his missed opportunities on earth to change the course of his eternal destiny. In the story of the rich man and Lazarus, the wealthy man begs for mercy upon his arrival in Hades. However, Abraham explains that any opportunity for relief from his agony is over:

> Child, *remember* that during your life you received your good things. (Luke 16:25)

The rich man will be haunted for all eternity by the memory of his life on earth—a life filled with underserved blessings from God and missed opportunities for a relationship with God. Perhaps the most painful aspect of hell will not be the unquenchable fire or blazing brimstone but the eternal lament of "if only."

Although there is an impassable gulf between hell and heaven, no such chasm appears between our life on earth and our existence in heaven or hell. One writer explains,

> Earth leads directly into heaven, just as it leads directly into hell. Life here is a running start into one or the other. Heaven and hell are both retroactive to earth. The best of earth is a glimpse of heaven, the worst of earth a glimpse of hell. Earth is the in between world touched both by heaven and hell, affording a choice between the two.[13]

Heaven Is Reserved for Those Who Trust in Christ

Andrew Sullivan, writing in *Newsweek*, argues that the Christian gospel has been corrupted through the years by those with political and financial agendas, and that we must return to the pure sayings of Jesus to rediscover the true gospel.

Yet in the same article, Sullivan claims that the New Testament was composed by "fallible men with fallible memories."[14] If that's true, then how could we ever determine which sayings of Jesus are authentic? If Jesus' claim to be equal to God (John 10:30) was nothing more than a manufactured quote by an overzealous scribe who sought to deify Jesus of Nazareth, then why do we automatically accept Jesus' teaching to "treat people the same way you want them to treat you" (Matthew 7:12)? If you can't trust all of Jesus' words in the Bible as authoritative, by what objective standard do you accept any of them?

But the converse is also true. If you accept some of Jesus' sayings, why not accept all of His teaching on all subjects as authoritative—which brings us to the seminal question of this chapter: how can I know I'm going to heaven when I die?

If you believe that there is strong evidence both inside and outside the Bible for life after death, and if you conclude that Jesus' teachings about heaven and hell offer the most reliable information about the possible destinations that await us when we die, then it only makes sense that you would also embrace Jesus' teachings about the way you can be assured of going to heaven when you die.

During His time on earth Jesus clearly explained how His followers could escape the reality of hell and experience heaven:

Truly, truly, I say to you, he who hears My word, and believes Him who sent Me has eternal life, and does not come into judgment, but has passed out of death into life. (John 5:24)

For this is the will of My Father, that everyone who beholds the Son and believes in Him will have eternal life, and I Myself will raise him up on the last day. (John 6:40)

> I am the resurrection and the life; he who believes in Me will live
> even if he dies. (John 11:25)

Jesus' teaching is clear: only those who believe in Jesus can be assured of heaven when they die. Obviously, a correct understanding of the word *believe* is critical here. Our eternal destiny hangs on this one word. To believe in Jesus does not mean to intellectually embrace certain facts about Jesus: He was the Son of God, He was crucified on a cross for the sins of the world, and He rose from the dead. Frankly, Satan and his demons believe those facts about Jesus—perhaps more than you and I do since they witnessed them firsthand!

To believe in Jesus means to trust in, adhere to, or cling to Jesus for the forgiveness of our sins. The starting place for that belief is the realization that we have disobeyed God in numerous ways and deserve His punishment. Nothing we have to offer—our relative goodness compared to other people, our religious rituals, our promises to do better—can ever earn us an acquittal from God from the eternal death sentence we deserve. Only when we are driven by desperation to depend upon Jesus Christ's death on the cross as sufficient payment for our sin can we know for sure we will be welcomed into heaven. Jesus explained it this way:

> For God so loved the world, that He gave His only begotten Son,
> that whoever believes in Him shall not perish, but have eternal
> life. (John 3:16)

Jesus declared that the only way to escape hell was to believe in Him. Since our eternal destiny hinges on that phrase, perhaps this illustration will help you understand what it means to believe in Him for the forgiveness of your sins.

Men, imagine taking your wife out to dinner at the most exclusive restaurant in town. You've been saving up for weeks for this special evening. You arrive at the restaurant dressed in nice, but casual clothes. When you check in with the maître d', he gives you the once-over, frowns, and points to a sign on the check-in podium that says, "Jackets Required."

You protest that there is nothing wrong with your attire and, furthermore, you had no prior knowledge of the restaurant's dress code. The maître d' tries to appease you by saying that you are not the only customer who has faced this predicament and offers you a jacket the restaurant keeps on hand for situations like this. Holding out the jacket, the maître d' asks, "Would you like to borrow our jacket?"

At that moment, you have a decision to make. You can acknowledge that your clothing does not meet the restaurant's requirements, put on the garment they offer, and enjoy a delicious dinner with your mate. Or you can refuse their offer and leave in a huff, saying, "If they don't accept me as I am, they will have to do without my business" and miss a fabulous evening with your wife.

God has a "dress code" for heaven. We must be wearing absolute perfection to be welcomed into His presence for eternity. Of course, none of us has perfection hanging in our closets. In fact, the Bible says our very best spiritual clothes are "like a filthy garment" in God's sight (Isaiah 64:6).

However, God has made a provision for our predicament. He offers to allow us to put on the righteousness of His Son Jesus Christ and enjoy an eternal celebration with Himself. What an offer! To believe in Jesus means to trust in the fact that Jesus took the rap or punishment for our unrighteousness when He died on the cross so that we can wrap ourselves in His perfection. Paul explained God's offer to exchange our sin with Christ's perfection this way:

> [God] made [Jesus] who knew no sin to be sin on our behalf, so that we might become the righteousness of God in Him. (2 Corinthians 5:21)

But to take advantage of that offer, we must first understand our need for that offer. And that requires humility.

You can either approach God dressed in your self-manufactured garment of good works, hoping that it is good enough to merit entrance into that eternal celebration God has planned. Or, you can believe what God says about the inadequacy of our goodness and receive the garment of perfection from Jesus Christ He offers you.

Before his confrontation with Jesus on the Damascus road, the apostle Paul was self-confident that as a "Hebrew of Hebrews" (Philippians 3:5), his spiritual clothing was superior to most. However, his face-to-face meeting with Jesus Christ (Acts 9:3–6) immediately changed his evaluation of himself. From that moment until the day Paul died, his prayer was that he

> may be found in [Christ], not having a righteousness of my own derived from the Law, but that which is through faith in Christ, the righteousness which comes from God on the basis of faith. (Philippians 3:9)

What about you? Which garment do you want to be wearing when the day arrives for you to face God? Waiting until you die to decide is too late. The only way you can be sure that you will be welcomed into heaven is by receiving God's offer of forgiveness on this side of the grave.

CHAPTER SIX

HOW CAN I KNOW HOW TO FORGIVE SOMEONE WHO HAS HURT ME?

I'm supposed to know a lot about forgiveness. I regularly preach about the subject to my congregation, I am interviewed about forgiveness in the national media, and I've written a best-selling book on the topic. I'm an expert on the subject of forgiveness . . . until it comes to actually having to forgive someone. A few days ago I was forced to realize just how bad of a forgiver I really am. While sitting in my car in the parking lot of a supermarket and talking on my cell phone, I noticed a man in a Hummer weaving through the lot in search of a shortcut to the bank adjacent to the supermarket. As he attempted to navigate his vehicle in the space between my car and one diagonal to mine, I gave a polite tap of the horn to alert him to the possibility of a collision.

Suddenly, the Hummer stopped and an oversized man bounded out of the driver's seat heading for my car. I have never seen anyone so angry. He began cursing and yelling and pounding on my window. "What's wrong with you? Why did you honk your horn? Get out of the car now!"

A verse from the Bible popped into my mind: "A gentle answer turns away wrath" (Proverbs 15:1). I thought this would be a good time to see if the verse really worked. So without lowering the window

(I wasn't *that* sure the verse would remedy the situation), I calmly explained through the window why I honked the horn, smiling the whole time. As I kept talking, he kept pounding. Finally, he turned away (yes, it does work), got in his vehicle, and parked in front of the bank. I sat in my car and watched him get out of his Hummer, *still* seething with anger over an innocuous honking of a horn.

Throughout the rest of the day I kept replaying the incident over in my mind and fantasizing about what I should have done. I'm ashamed to put this in print for posterity, but I actually created a mental scenario in which I suddenly put my car in reverse and, just as my would-be assailant thought I was leaving, suddenly sped toward him and pinned him against the bumper of his car. But that wasn't all. As he writhed in pain, I imagined putting my car in reverse and using it as a motorized battering ram, striking a second blow, and a third, and . . . well, you get the idea. My difficulty in letting go of that incident reminds me of C. S. Lewis's observation that "forgiveness is a lovely idea, until [you] have something to forgive."[1]

I suspect there is someone in your past who has deeply hurt you. It may be an employer who wronged you, a friend who betrayed you, a parent who abused you, or a mate who deserted you. While your thoughts of revenge against that person may not be as violent as mine, you still have difficulty releasing the hurt you experienced. And honestly, you're not sure if you *should* let go. After all, doesn't your offender deserve to pay for what he has done to you?

In my experience as a pastor no decision is more difficult or more crucial than choosing to forgive those who wrong us. Author David Augsburger observes that forgiveness is hard, it hurts, and it costs.[2] But the decision not to forgive is even more costly.

WHY FORGIVENESS MATTERS

Until fairly recently, the subject of forgiveness was relegated to a Sunday school nicety that was as universally acknowledged and routinely ignored as Jesus' admonition to turn the other cheek. *Such reactions to mistreatment may work in a perfect world, but certainly not in my world,* many of us conclude. Yet over the last few decades researchers have uncovered convincing evidence of the physical and emotional benefits of forgiveness.

Recently I toured the Holocaust Museum in Jerusalem. There are no words to describe the horror the Jewish people endured at the hands of their Nazi tormentors. I understand the sentiment of one Jewish survivor of that nightmare who declared, "If you could lick my heart, it would poison you."[3] Yet that is exactly the problem. Unforgiveness is a deadly toxin in our bodies resulting in real and measurable physiological effects. Respected psychologist Dr. Glen Mack Harnden writes that forgiveness releases us "from prolonged anger, rage, and stress that have been linked to physiological problems, such as cardiovascular diseases, high blood pressure, hypertension, cancer, and other psychosomatic illnesses."[4]

Forgiveness is also crucial for our emotional health. A popular television drama, *Revenge*, chronicles a young woman's intricate plan to avenge her father's unjust imprisonment and death. Every week viewers watch her coldly devise and execute a plan to destroy the lives of those who wronged her father. Each new episode begins with the same flashback of the woman—then a little girl—watching her father being arrested and hauled off to prison as she screams in anguish, "Daddy, Daddy!"

While the weekly recap is for the benefit of new viewers to the program, it also is a vivid reminder of the downside of bitterness. When we choose to hold on to an offense rather than release it, we are choosing to mentally replay that painful episode and relive its resulting hurt. Allowing someone to injure us once may be unavoidable, but who in his right mind would choose to allow that same person to continue assaulting us?

However, forgiveness is the process by which we let go of a painful experience—and the one who caused it—for our own emotional benefit. Forgiveness is like letting go of a rattlesnake. The choice benefits the snake, but it benefits us even more! Lewis Smedes writes, "To forgive is to put down your 50-pound pack after a 10-mile climb up a mountain. To forgive is to fall into a chair after a 15-mile marathon. To forgive is to set a prisoner free and discover the prisoner was you."[5]

But the physical and emotional results of forgiveness pale in significance to the spiritual benefits of releasing those who have wronged us. Simply put: if you are unwilling to forgive others, God will not forgive you. Jesus made that claim in Matthew 6:14–15:

> For if you forgive others for their transgressions, your heavenly Father will also forgive you. But if you do not forgive others, then your Father will not forgive your transgressions.

I've always been troubled by people who claim to believe in the inspiration of the Bible, yet try to diminish or dismiss Jesus' clear teaching in this passage. "What Jesus *meant* to say was . . ."

Jesus could not have spoken more clearly. There is an inseparable link between forgiving others and being forgiven by God. Is Christ suggesting that we earn God's forgiveness by forgiving other people? No, for that would mean that grace is earned rather than received as a gift. "For by grace you have been saved through faith; and that not of yourselves, it is the gift of God; not as a result of works, so that no one may boast," the apostle Paul declared (Ephesians 2:8–9).

Perhaps Jesus is saying that our forgiveness, though received as a gift, can be revoked if we refuse to forgive others. But that possibility would also contradict the Bible's teaching that "the gifts and calling of God are irrevocable" (Romans 11:29). So how is our willingness to forgive others coupled with God's willingness to forgive us?

Jesus answered that question in a famous parable about a slave who owed his king a debt of ten thousand talents (one talent equaled approximately eighty pounds of gold), which in today's currency would have amounted to around five billion dollars! When the king demanded repayment from his servant, the slave begged the king for mercy. When the king saw his servant prostrate before him, Jesus said, "the lord of that slave felt compassion and released him and forgave him the debt" (Matthew 18:27).

One can only imagine the relief the slave felt when he heard the king say, "Your debt is forgiven." Yet, amazingly, this forgiven slave went out and found a fellow slave who owed him a measly hundred denarii, which would amount to about sixteen dollars today. When the second slave pleaded for mercy, the first slave refused to grant the same grace that he had just received from the king and instead had him thrown into debtors' prison. When word of the incident reached the king's ears, the king was incensed and demanded that the unforgiving slave be brought before him.

> "You wicked slave, I forgave you all that debt because you pleaded with me. Should you not also have had mercy on your fellow slave, in the same way that I had mercy on you?" And his lord, moved with anger, handed him over to the torturers until he should repay all that was owed him. (Matthew 18:32–34)

The king could not believe that a slave who had been forgiven a multibillion-dollar debt would be unwilling to forgive the paltry sixteen-dollar debt owed a fellow slave. Sure, the first slave had a legal right to his sixteen dollars. However, given the huge debt from which he had been released, the first slave had no moral right to demand repayment. Granting forgiveness should be a natural response to receiving forgiveness, the king reasoned as he ordered the imprisonment of the unforgiving slave. Then Jesus closed with this application:

> My heavenly Father will also do the same to you, if each of you does not forgive his brother from your heart. (Matthew 18:35)

In my experience as a pastor I've heard professing Christians adamantly declare, "I will never forgive that person for what he did to me." Does such a refusal to forgive cause God to rescind the forgiveness He has already granted the nonforgiver? No, but it is an indication that the nonforgiver has never truly received God's forgiveness. Kathy Dahlen writes,

> Unforgiving people are consumed with their own circumstances and feelings. The sad result is an arrogant denial of God's mercy, trivializing God's own great sacrifice. Their sense of personal wrong (however warranted) so fills their vision that they cannot see beyond it to the cross. Unforgiving people cannot be truly contrite before God in response to their own sins.[6]

If we truly understood the tremendous debt from which God had forgiven us, we would be more inclined to extend that same forgiveness to others. Jesus is not denying the reality of the indescribable pain of betrayal and abuse that we experience at the hands of other people, but He is reminding us to keep such pain in perspective. The difference between how much others have wronged us and we have wronged God is the difference between sixteen dollars and five billion dollars.

Only when we understand the size of the debt we owe God will we be motivated to prostrate ourselves before Him and beg for His forgiveness. And then—and only then—will we be willing to show similar mercy to others who wrong us. It is extremely difficult to give away what you have not first received.

UNDERSTANDING WHAT FORGIVENESS IS . . . AND ISN'T

In spite of the incalculable physical, emotional, and spiritual benefits of releasing rather than holding on to the hurts of others, our first— and far too often, final—response to those offenses is unforgiveness. Given the corrosive effects of bitterness on our bodies and emotions, not to mention the spiritual hazards of unforgiveness, why are we so reluctant to forgive those who wrong us?

Some might argue that because of our inherited predisposition to sin we are naturally wired to retaliate against those who attack us. The Latin phrase *lex talionis*, or "the law of the talon," recognizes humans' instinct to strike back against those who wrong us. Our inborn propensity toward vengeance explains why several of man's earliest codes of law were built upon the premise of an eye for an eye and a tooth for a tooth (Exodus 21:24). However, if that principle were taken to its natural end all of society would end up blind and toothless! As one writer notes, forgiveness allows us to "step off the escalator of revenge so that both of us can stop the chain of incremental wrongs."[7] Forgiveness is a way to hit the reset button in a relationship and put an end to the destructive cycle of retaliation.

Unfortunately, many people are unwilling or unable to hit that reset button of forgiveness because they don't know what it looks like. I believe that the major reason people are reluctant to forgive other people is that they have a faulty understanding of what forgiveness is . . . and what it is not.

Forgiveness Is Not Ignoring or Rationalizing

One reason people are hesitant to forgive is that they wrongly equate forgiveness with ignoring or diminishing the seriousness of an offense. How can anyone sweep under the rug physical abuse by a mate, sexual molestation by a parent, or the death of a child by a drunk driver?

To forgive someone does not require that we engage in some mental fantasy, pretending the offense never happened. In fact, it is impossible to truly forgive an offense unless we first acknowledge the reality and the seriousness of the wrong committed. As someone has said, we can only forgive those whom we are willing to blame.

I think Christians try to be far too nice when it comes to holding people accountable for their offenses. We know we are supposed to forgive those who hurt us, so we try to ignore or rationalize the pain we feel from the offense.

"Oh, I'm sure he didn't mean it."

"I realize I'm just as much a part of the problem as she is."

"He was probably just having a bad day."

The problem with ignoring or rationalizing the offenses of others is that it short-circuits the process of forgiveness, which is vital to our physical, emotional, and spiritual healing. For example, suppose you notice a bump on your right arm that begins to hurt. At first, you try to ignore the pain. Then you rationalize that it probably came from inadvertently running into a door and will eventually go away. You devise every excuse imaginable for not seeing a physician. Then, one day the pain is so intense you schedule an appointment with your doctor. But it's too late. The tumor on your arm has metastasized and spread throughout your body. "If only you had come in earlier, we could have removed this and saved your life," your doctor laments.

Forgiveness is a surgical procedure that allows us to remove the tumor of bitterness from our souls. However, before we can excise the tumor, we first have to acknowledge that it exists. The story of Joseph in the Old Testament, which we briefly discussed in the previous chapter, is one of the greatest examples of forgiveness in history. In case you have forgotten the story, let me recap it for you.

Joseph was sold into slavery by his brothers, who were jealous of their father's favoritism toward him. Through a series of God-directed circumstances, Joseph arose to be Pharaoh's right-hand man in Egypt. Eventually, a great famine forced Joseph's brothers to travel to Egypt to buy food. Little did they know that the man from whom they would be requesting food was their own brother, whom they had assumed was dead.

When the brothers realized Joseph was not only alive and standing before them but also possessed the authority to extinguish their lives with a single command, they were filled with fear. However,

Joseph surprised them by his response. He not only forgave his brothers but he offered them the most fertile land of Egypt in which to reside.

Years later, after their father, Jacob, died, the brothers feared that Joseph might finally seek retribution from his brothers for his mistreatment. However, Joseph relieved their anxiety by explaining why he was willing to let go of what could have been an all-consuming bitterness over his mistreatment:

> As for you, you meant evil against me, but God meant it for good in order to bring about this present result, to preserve many people alive. So therefore, do not be afraid; I will provide for you and your little ones. (Genesis 50:20–21)

Notice that Joseph in no way ignored or rationalized his brothers' treachery. He didn't say, "You and I were both wrong. Had I not flaunted our father's obvious favoritism toward me, perhaps you would not have reacted the way you did." Joseph was not hesitant to lay the blame completely at his brothers' feet. "You meant evil."

But Joseph was able to look beyond his brothers' evil motives and see the hand of an all-powerful God who was able to use their mistreatment for good. Forgiveness is made easier by belief in a sovereign God, but it always begins with an acknowledgment of wrong. We can only forgive those we are willing to blame.

Forgiveness Is Not Surrendering Our Desire for Justice

The teenage daughter of a former church member of mine was brutally murdered. The killer was apprehended, and the prosecutors wanted the father to testify at the trial. "I am struggling with forgiving this man for what he did to my daughter, but I'm really trying. If I testify at the trial against him, isn't that an indication that I am unwilling to forgive him?" the father asked me.

I explained to him the difference between vengeance and justice. Vengeance is the desire to hurt those who have hurt us (like repeatedly ramming with an automobile someone who has tried to assault you!). The Bible warns us against avenging those who wrong us:

Never take your own revenge, beloved, but leave room for the wrath of God, for it is written, "VENGEANCE IS MINE, I WILL REPAY," says the Lord. (Romans 12:19)

First Samuel 26 records a fascinating story about a time when David had the opportunity to kill his arch-nemesis King Saul, who had tried numerous times to destroy the up-and-coming leader of Israel. Yet David's men were dismayed by his unwillingness to take advantage of a perfect opportunity to end Saul's life while he lay sleeping. David explained his reason for refusing to seek vengeance:

"Do not destroy him, for who can stretch out his hand against the LORD's anointed and be without guilt?" David also said, "As the LORD lives, surely the LORD will strike him, or his day will come that he dies, or he will go down into battle and perish." (1 Samuel 26:9–10)

David never said to his men, "Saul isn't such a bad guy. If you really understood him, you would feel differently toward him." David knew Saul deserved the death sentence for his actions. But David trusted in God to deal with Saul in His own way and according to His own timetable, which He eventually did. First Samuel 31 records that Saul chose to take his own life rather than suffer an ignominious death at the hand of the Philistines. When the Philistines discovered his body, they cut off Saul's head and hung his body from a wall at Beth-shan for all to see. This story is a powerful reminder that God is much more capable of settling the score with our enemies than we are.

But while we are commanded not to seek vengeance—hurting others for hurting us—we cannot and should not surrender our desire for justice. Since we are created in the image of a righteous God who hates evil and punishes evildoers, it is only natural that we would desire to see child abusers incarcerated and murderers executed. Justice is the payment God or others demand from those who wrong us or other people. The Bible extols the desire for justice:

Do justice to the afflicted and destitute. (Psalm 82:3)

Seek justice, reprove the ruthless, defend the orphan, plead for the widow. (Isaiah 1:17)

And what does the LORD require of you but to do justice, to love kindness, and to walk humbly with your God? (Micah 6:8)

The difference between vengeance and justice is crucial to being able to forgive other people. For example, suppose I had told the father of the murdered teenager that in order to truly forgive his daughter's killer, he would have to surrender any desire to see the murderer punished for his actions. That would be both an impossible and unnecessary demand that could be a barrier preventing the father from experiencing the healing power of forgiveness. The father's desire to see his daughter's killer pay for his crime is not the result of his sin nature, but of his God-like nature. To ask him to give up his desire for justice is both impossible and unnecessary.

Instead, I explained to that father that forgiveness meant surrendering his right to get even ("an eye for an eye") and trusting God to punish his daughter's killer, which God often does through the judicial system. In Romans 13, the apostle Paul explains that government serves as "a minister of God, an avenger who brings wrath on the one who practices evil" (Romans 13:4). Forgiveness means giving up our desire for vengeance, not our desire for justice.

Forgiveness Is Not Forgetting Offenses

Many people wrongly assume that truly forgiving another person requires forgetting the offense the person has committed against us. Such a demand erects another unnecessary hurdle that prevents people from experiencing the healing benefits of forgiveness for several reasons.

First, asking someone to forget the hurt he has endured is often viewed as tantamount to denying the seriousness of the offense. Try saying to a survivor of the Holocaust who saw her child taken to the crematorium, "You need to forget about that and get on with your life." To ask a mother to forget such a horror would be to diminish the seriousness of the crime and the value of her child's life.

Additionally, telling people they must forget an offense is asking them to do something that is impossible. Occasionally someone will say to me, "I thought I had truly forgiven that person for what he did to me, but I guess I haven't because I still think about it." I remind that person that forgiving is a spiritual function, but forgetting is a biological function. Memories are imbedded in our brain through a combination of chemical and electronic impulses. Although we cannot always recall certain experiences at will (like where we placed our car keys), those memories are still in our brain and could resurface at any time. It is impossible for people to perform a "memory wipe" of their brain.

However, forgiveness is a spiritual function in which a victim chooses to surrender any right for revenge and entrusts God with the responsibility for dealing justly with the wrongdoer. When I teach this very real distinction between forgiving and forgetting, someone invariably says, "But doesn't the Bible say that when God forgives, He also forgets? Shouldn't we model our forgiveness of others after God's forgiveness of us?"

It is true that the Bible appears to equate God's forgiveness of our sins with His forgetting our sins:

He will again have compassion on us; He will tread our iniquities under foot. Yes, You will cast all their sins into the depths of the sea. (Micah 7:19)

For I will forgive their iniquity, and their sin I will remember no more. (Jeremiah 31:34)

But is it really possible for an omniscient (meaning "all-knowing") God to suddenly develop a case of heavenly Alzheimer's and actually forget what we have done? These verses are best understood as what theologians call "anthropomorphisms"—attempts to explain the actions of an infinite God to finite man using concepts with which we are familiar. These verses are meant to assure us that once God has forgiven us, we never have to worry that at some point in the future He will dredge up some past transgression and say, "I know I told you I've forgiven you for this, but on second thought . . ."

The New Testament explains more fully what happens to our sins when we receive God's forgiveness. Quoting Psalm 32, Paul wrote to the Roman Christians:

Blessed are those whose lawless deeds have been forgiven, and whose sins have been covered. Blessed is the man whose sin the Lord will not take into account. (Romans 4:7–8)

When we wrong someone—whether that someone is another person or God—we automatically become indebted to him for our offense. Sin always creates an obligation. Our offenses against God are so serious and numerous that the Bible declares, "The wages of sin is death" (Romans 6:23). We deserve to die eternally because of the transgressions we have committed against our Creator. However, when we trust in Jesus Christ as our Savior, God views Christ's death on the cross as sufficient payment for our spiritual debt.

Colossians 2 explains the spiritual transaction that takes place when someone chooses to receive Christ's payment for his sins, rather than choosing to spend all eternity paying off that debt himself:

> . . . having forgiven us all our transgressions, having canceled out the certificate of debt consisting of decrees against us, which was hostile to us; and He has taken it out of the way; having nailed it to the cross. (vv. 13–14)

The bottom-line result of Christ's death is that our "certificate of debt" has been marked "paid in full," meaning that we never have to worry that God is going to come after us like an irate bill collector seeking payment for a debt that has already been fulfilled. God will no longer take into account our sin debt because it has already been paid.

However, forgiving debt does not necessitate forgetting debt. For example, before I could sell our first home to a buyer, I had to provide proof to the bank that I had indeed paid off a second mortgage held by another lending institution. The bank did not want to give me the proceeds of the sale until I could prove that the debt had been satisfied. Fortunately, the other lending institution had not "forgotten" my debt. They were able to retrieve a copy of it, even though the debt had been forgiven. Even though they had retained a copy of the mortgage that had been paid off, I never once worried that the record of that past debt would cause the lending institution to demand payment from me again.

God's forgiveness of our sins should erase any fear that He will demand payment from us for a debt that has already been paid by His own Son. Although God does not technically forget that debt, He never again charges it against our spiritual account. Similarly, when we forgive another person who has wronged us, we are surrendering our right to collect what that person owes us. Anytime we remember that debt, we are also to remember that we have turned that debt over to God to collect in His own way and in His own time.

Forgiveness Is Not Reconciling with Our Offender

One of the greatest misunderstandings about forgiveness is that truly letting go of an offense results in immediate reconciliation with the person who has hurt us. In fact, some people claim that you cannot truly forgive someone unless you are willing to be reunited with your offender, even at the risk of being wronged again. After all, didn't Jesus demand that we be willing to forgive others "seventy times seven" (Matthew 18:22)?

If reconciliation is a condition for genuine forgiveness, then you can understand why some people are reluctant to forgive. Imagine a wife, separated from her husband because of years of intense physical abuse, being told that if she has truly forgiven her husband she will move back into his house and place her life in jeopardy. How eager is she going to be to forgive her mate? Or consider a man who was sexually abused as a child by an uncle being told that if he has truly forgiven his uncle he will be willing to allow his own children to visit that uncle. "After all, the Bible says that love always trusts," the man's pastor reminds him.

Certainly reestablishing a relationship with someone who has wronged us is a desirable goal that should not be diminished in any way. After all, when God forgives us of our sins He doesn't say, "Although I have surrendered My right to punish you, I never want to have anything to do with you. You go your way, and I'll go Mine." One of God's motivations for forgiving our sins was that He might enjoy an eternal relationship with us.

In the same way, God desires that we rebuild broken relationships with those who have wronged us. The Bible consistently extols the value of reconciliation with our enemies:

Behold, how good and how pleasant it is for brothers to dwell together in unity! (Psalm 133:1)

. . . being diligent to preserve the unity of the Spirit in the bond of peace. There is one body and one Spirit, just as also you were called in one hope of your calling. (Ephesians 4:3–4)

Make my joy complete by being of the same mind, maintaining the same love, united in spirit, intent on one purpose. (Philippians 2:2)

Although reconciliation between Christians is a preferred outcome, it is not always possible. The apostle Paul advised the Roman Christians, "*If possible*, so far as it depends on you, be at peace with all men" (Romans 12:18).

The restoration of a broken relationship doesn't always depend on us. For example, if you cheat on your mate you can ask for forgiveness—which your spouse may or may not grant. Even if your mate decides to forgive you, she may choose to dissolve the marriage. As much as you may desire to reconcile with your wounded partner, the ultimate decision rests with her.

Similarly, when someone wrongs us, we can and should immediately and completely forgive our offender, utilizing the process that I will discuss in the next section. However, while forgiveness is a unilateral action without any conditions, reconciliation is a mutual decision between us and our offender that demands the fulfillment of several conditions.

First, my offender must demonstrate *repentance*. Until he is willing to admit he has wronged me, I will have difficulty ever reestablishing a relationship with him. Why? The foundation of any relationship is common agreement. The prophet Amos asked, "Can two walk together, except they be agreed?" (Amos 3:3 KJV). Amos is not suggesting that we have to agree with someone about every issue to enjoy a relationship with him. Friends, business associates, church members, and marriage partners can enjoy satisfying relationships and still disagree about issues ranging from theology to thermostat settings.

However, it is impossible to maintain an intimate relationship with someone with whom you have a fundamental disagreement over an issue of great importance. And no issue is any more important to us than our mistreatment by another person. If a husband wounds his wife with a critical observation, the result will be an emotional breach in the relationship no matter how much the husband claims, "That was no big deal." As long as the husband and wife disagree over whether his comments were "a big deal," then emotional reconciliation will be difficult to establish.

Rehabilitation is also another reasonable prerequisite for reconciliation. When I've talked with women who have been physically battered by their husbands, I encourage them to let go of their desire to hurt their mates for hurting them. Bitterness only further damages the victim of abuse. However, I am quick to remind the abused wife that she can forgive her husband without moving back in with him. If he is truly sorry for what he has done, he will take steps to change his behavior, such as seeking the help of a Christian counselor.

Rehabilitation always begins with repentance. The word *repent* means "to turn around" and involves a change of mind that leads to a change of direction (or rehabilitation). Paul reminded the Corinthian Christians that there is a difference between emotional sorrow and genuine sorrow:

For the sorrow that is according to the will of God produces a repentance without regret, leading to salvation. (2 Corinthians 7:10)

A physically abusive husband whose wife has moved out may be sorry that he no longer has someone to cook his meals, wash his clothes, and sleep in his bed. However, if the husband is truly repentant he will be sorry enough about his actions and the resulting consequences to change his behavior.

Restoring a broken relationship may also require *restitution*. You may forgive a business partner who has cheated you out of fifty thousand dollars. You may choose to turn your case over to the legal system for justice, trusting God to render an equitable verdict instead of personally settling the score with him for his dishonesty. However, suppose after several years your former partner approaches you and says, "I would like for us to go back into business together." You express your hesitation, to which he counters, "I'm a changed person and, after all, you said you have forgiven me." Your natural response would be, "If you've really changed, where's the fifty thousand dollars you stole from me?" In a case like this, restitution is the most powerful evidence of genuine repentance.

"But Robert, doesn't forgiveness mean giving up our demand for repayment?" Yes, but we are not talking about forgiveness but about reconciliation. While revenge is the payment we *demand* from our offender, restitution is the payment our offender *volunteers* to effect reconciliation.

Remember the story of the notorious tax collector Zacchaeus recorded in the New Testament? After he received Jesus' forgiveness he voluntarily made this offer:

Zacchaeus stopped and said to the Lord, "Behold, Lord, half of my possessions I will give to the poor, and if I have defrauded anyone of anything, I will give back four times as much." And

Jesus said to him, "Today salvation has come to this house." (Luke 19:8–9)

Zacchaeus's willingness to repay those whom he had defrauded was not a condition to receiving Jesus' forgiveness but was evidence of his genuine repentance. While you can forgive someone who refuses to offer restitution for his offense, you are unwise to reestablish a relationship—especially one that involves money—with that person.

Understanding the difference between forgiveness and reconciliation is vital to overcoming one of the chief objections to releasing hurts in our life. We can and must forgive those who wrong us, but that forgiveness does not always result in a restored relationship with our offender.

- Forgiveness has no conditions; reconciliation has several conditions.
- Forgiveness can be offered to those who never admit they could be wrong; reconciliation can be offered only to those who admit they're wrong.
- Forgiveness depends upon me; reconciliation depends on us.

Now that we have discovered what forgiveness is not, it is important to understand what forgiveness is and how we can extend it to those who wrong us.

UNDERSTANDING GENUINE FORGIVENESS

When I was growing up, I remember hearing my father and mother argue about money occasionally. "If you keep spending like this, we are going to end up in the poorhouse!" my dad would warn my mom. As a little boy I had no idea what the poorhouse was, but I assumed it was not a place in which I wanted to spend any amount of time.

My father's warning was an allusion to the debtors' prisons of another era. Centuries ago, if you could not pay your bills you went to prison until your bills were repaid. However, the practice had one serious flaw: if you were in prison, how could you ever hope to repay your debt? The end result of this system of "justice" was that the debtor died, his family starved, and the debt holder went unpaid.

I think the king in Jesus' parable who was owed five billion dollars by his slave understood the futility of debtors' prison. Jesus identified the king's compassion as his motivation for extending mercy to the slave. But the king's compassion was most likely fueled by common sense.

Seeing the slave prostrate before him begging for mercy and promising to repay the huge debt caused the king to realize his options were limited. Incarcerating the slave would not reduce his debt by a single denarius. Releasing the servant from prison but insisting that he repay the debt on an installment plan was equally unrealistic ("We are going to take a little out of your paycheck every week until the entire five billion is repaid—which by our calculations will be in two hundred million years.")

If imprisonment was futile and repayment was unrealistic, then the only sensible choice was to forgive the debt, which is exactly what the king chose to do:

> And the lord of that slave felt compassion and released him and forgave him the debt. (Matthew 18:27)

The two words Jesus uses to describe the king's actions are crucial to understanding what genuine forgiveness entails. The Greek word *apoluo* is translated "released" and it means "to let go of" or "to set at liberty." The second word, *aphiemi*, is a financial term that means "to cancel a debt."

The two words Jesus utilizes here—and the order in which He uses them—are neither redundant nor accidental. The word translated "released" comes immediately after "compassion" and describes an emotional decision. Compassion (coupled with common sense) compelled the king to surrender his insistence for repayment of the debt. That emotion-based decision resulted in a practical result: the forgiving or canceling of the servant's debt.

The king's action toward his servant illustrates the three necessary steps for experiencing the benefits of this spiritual transaction called forgiveness.

Genuine Forgiveness Acknowledges the Offense

Never in this parable is there a suggestion that the servant's debt was imaginary or illegitimate. Jesus said that the servant "owed him" (Matthew 18:24). Acknowledging the reality of a wrong is no small issue when it comes to the process of forgiveness. You cannot release someone from a debt that does not exist. Likewise, you cannot forgive someone of a wrong that has not occurred. You can only forgive those you are willing to blame.

I'm often asked if it is necessary for us to confront our offender in order to acknowledge the wrong that has occurred. After all, didn't Joseph confront his brothers who sold him into slavery with his famous words "You meant evil against me, but God meant it for good" (Genesis 50:20)? Is personal confrontation a necessary prerequisite for forgiveness?

I believe it is clear from Joseph's words that he had already forgiven his brothers by the time he revealed his identity to them. Joseph had obviously spent many years reflecting on how God had used his brothers' betrayal to fulfill His plan for his life. To be able to see God's hand in the hurts from another is only possible for those who have forgiven their offenders.

Joseph's purpose in acknowledging his brothers' sin was not to elicit repentance from them so that he could then forgive them. Instead, Joseph was trying to effect reconciliation with his family by eliminating any fear or embarrassment they might have harbored about their actions. Whether we confront our offender or not depends upon our motive. If we are hoping that such a confrontation will elicit an "I'm sorry," we may be setting ourselves up for disappointment. The person who has hurt us deeply may not realize or even care that he has injured us.

However, if our motive for confrontation is to pave the way for reconciliation with someone we have *already* truly forgiven, then it may be helpful to let that person know we have forgiven him and want to reestablish a relationship with him. But acknowledging the reality of an offense is always a vital first step in forgiveness, even if that acknowledgment occurs only in our own heart.

Genuine Forgiveness Calculates the Debt

Jesus did not merely say the servant owed the king a debt but specifically identified the amount of the debt: ten thousand talents. Before we can legitimately release someone of a debt we must clearly understand what that debt is.

Wrongs create an obligation. Running a red light results in a fine. Selling cocaine results in a prison term. Violating God's commands results in eternal separation from God. Although the policeman who stops us, the judge who sentences us, or the God against whom we rebel has latitude in how he deals with our transgression, the obligation is nevertheless real.

When Joseph said to his brothers, "Do not be afraid" (Genesis 50:19), he was implying that they had every right to be afraid! Their betrayal of their brother, who had become the second most powerful man in Egypt, was a capital crime that called for the death penalty. Before either we or our offender can appreciate the great freedom that comes from forgiveness, both the forgiver and the forgiven need to have a clear understanding of the debt from which the offender is being released.

When someone has been deeply wounded by another person, I often counsel him not to only acknowledge the wrong that has occurred but actually to specify the punishment the offender deserves:

- Because you betrayed me, you deserve to have our friendship end.
- Because you betrayed me by having an affair, you deserve a divorce.
- Because you abused me as a child, you deserve to spend the rest of your life in prison.
- Because you killed my child, you deserve to die.

I'm not suggesting that you should voice this to your offender—especially if he is unaware or uncaring about his actions. Getting into an argument with someone who has already hurt you about the reality or severity of that hurt is counterproductive to the forgiveness process. However, performing a mental calculation of your offender's obligation toward you is a crucial step in the forgiveness process. You can only release offenses you have acknowledged, and you can only cancel debts you have calculated.

Genuine Forgiveness Releases the Debtor to God

Unlike the king who "released" and "forgave" the servant of his titanic debt, the forgiven slave found a fellow slave who owed him a real, but relatively small, amount of money and "seized him and began to choke him" (Matthew 18:28). Unforgiveness refuses to let go. Unforgiveness retains a death grip on both the offender and the offense, trying to extract a payment that will in some way compensate for the injury we have sustained.

But usually our offender is incapable of making a payment sufficient to cover the wrong he has committed. What adequate restitution could someone offer us for a marriage ruined through adultery, a childhood innocence destroyed by incest, or a life snuffed out by negligent driving? Although an apology, a divorce, a prison term, or even a death sentence might offer temporary relief from our pain, it cannot provide permanent healing. Our offender is just as incapable of satisfying the debt he owes us as both slaves in Jesus' parable were of satisfying theirs.

The contrast in Jesus' story was in the actions of the debt holders. The king realized he was holding a worthless account receivable. No matter how hard and long he squeezed his slave, the slave would never be able to repay the debt. So the king did the only reasonable thing he could do: he released the slave, absorbed the loss himself, and got on with his life.

However, the first slave did not understand that his fellow slave was just as incapable of repaying the small debt he owed as he himself was in satisfying his large indebtedness to the king. Unlike the king, the first slave refused to release his fellow slave of the debt. He threw him into a debtors' prison until he repaid the debt—which, given his obvious inability to work while incarcerated, meant never. When the king heard about his slave's unwillingness to forgive such a minor sum—especially in light of the major obligation of which he had just been forgiven—the king had the unforgiving slave placed into prison until he repaid everything, which again meant never.

Prison is an apt metaphor in this story for describing the results of unforgiveness. By consigning his fellow slave to prison, the unforgiving slave was sentencing himself to prison as well. Ironically, his unwillingness to let go of his fellow slave's measly debt resulted in a lifetime of captivity for himself. Why would any sensible person surrender his own freedom in order to hold on to an uncollectible debt?

When we refuse to forgive other people, Jesus concluded, we risk spending eternity in the spiritual (but very real) prison of hell—all because of our refusal to release a fellow human being from a debt he or she is powerless to repay. But unforgiveness also has some immediate consequences in this life, as well.

When we refuse to release our offender, we enter into our own private prison in which we are emotionally chained to our offender and forced to repeatedly relive the hurt we have already experienced—all because we will not let go. It's like picking up the rattlesnake that bit you once and angrily squeezing it as it strikes you over and over.

Forgiveness means transferring to God our right to extract payment from our offender. A company that finds itself unable to collect a bill from a delinquent customer will turn that bill over to a debt collector. Similarly, when we forgive someone we are emotionally releasing him and assigning his obligation to the ultimate Debt Collector. Forgiveness does not require surrendering our desire for justice but surrendering our right to execute justice.

Michael Saward, a well-known evangelical Anglican, answered the front door of his London home one morning. Three strangers standing at the front door beat him over the head with a cricket bat and fractured his skull. The intruders then raped Saward's daughter and savagely beat the daughter's boyfriend. After the men were arrested, Saward expressed his forgiveness of his assailants in a television interview. However, after the trial Saward criticized the court for only giving his attackers three to five years in prison.[8] Although Michael Saward gave up his right to go after his assailants with his own cricket bat, he never surrendered his desire to see the justice system inflict its own punishment against the three men. As noted in the previous section, God often uses the church (1 Corinthians 5) or government (Romans 13:1–5) as instruments of His vengeance against wrongdoing.

I am frequently asked, "Can I forgive someone who does not ask to be forgiven?" Those who want to make repentance a condition for forgiveness point out that just as God's forgiveness is conditioned upon our repentance, we cannot—and should not—forgive someone who refuses to ask to be forgiven.

The flaw in that argument is a failure to recognize the difference between *receiving* forgiveness and *granting* forgiveness. It is true that I cannot receive forgiveness from God or another person until I realize I need that forgiveness. Only an open hand can receive a gift. As long as my heart is closed, unwilling to acknowledge my wrongdoing, I cannot receive grace from God or others.

However, I can grant forgiveness to anyone at any time, independent of that other person's actions or attitudes. Jesus illustrated the possibility of unconditional forgiveness when He commanded, "And whenever you stand praying, forgive, if you have anything against anyone, so that your Father who is in heaven will also forgive you your transgressions" (Mark 11:25). You have both the ability and responsibility to let go of that person who has hurt you deeply whether they are in the next room, another state, or the cemetery.

The spiritual motivation for unconditional forgiveness is the realization of that tremendous debt of sin from which God has forgiven you. The practical motivation for unconditional forgiveness is the freedom that comes from letting go of the offender and the offense that has brought so much pain into your life.

Conditioning your forgiveness upon your offender's actions—repentance, rehabilitation, restitution—is to willingly remain in the position of a victim. I compare conditional forgiveness to one of those three-legged races people used to participate in at picnics. You bind your leg to your partner's as you hobble together toward the finish line. Everyone on the sidelines hoots and hollers as they watch you awkwardly trying to move forward. You could run a lot faster on your own, but three-legged races do not allow for solo contenders. You are bound to your partner. You can move only as far and as fast as your partner is able to run.

When you make your forgiveness of another person dependent on the actions of your offender, you remain emotionally bound to the person who has wronged you. You can travel no further or faster in life than he does. If he refuses to say "I'm sorry" or demonstrate his remorse by some change in his actions or attitudes, you are destined to hobble through life together. However, by unconditionally forgiving that person you are saying, "Although what you did to me was wrong, I am letting go of that wrong so that I can be free to get on with my life." Forgiveness benefits us much more than it benefits our offender.

On April 18, 1942, Lt. Col. James H. Doolittle led a bombing raid over Japan, the first such offensive mission since the Japanese attack on Pearl Harbor a few months earlier. On its return to the aircraft carrier one of the planes ran out of fuel, forcing the five crewmen to bail out over Japanese-occupied territory in China. They were quickly captured by the Japanese, and two of the crewmen were executed by a firing squad. The remaining three airmen spent the next forty months being starved, beaten, and tortured by the Japanese. Among those American soldiers was Corporal Jacob DeShazer.

DeShazer recalled that during his captivity he had one source of comfort: "I begged my captors to get a Bible for me. At last a guard brought me the book, but told me I could have it only for three weeks. I eagerly began to read its pages. I discovered that God had given me spiritual eyes and that when I looked at the enemy officers and guards who had starved and beaten my companions and me so cruelly, I found my bitter hatred for them changed to loving pity. I realized that these people did not know anything about my Savior and that if Christ is not in a heart, it is natural to be cruel,"[9] DeShazer later said. Corporal DeShazer determined that if he survived the ordeal he would spend the rest of his life sharing Christ's message of love and forgiveness with everyone he could. After the end of the war, DeShazer followed through on his commitment and spent thirty years in Japan as a missionary.

One day Mitsuo Fuchida, the Japanese naval flier who had led the attack against Pearl Harbor, stumbled upon a booklet written by DeShazer describing his ordeal in the Japanese prison and his decision to forgive his Japanese torturers. Fuchida said, "It was then that I met Jesus and accepted him as my Savior." Over the intervening years Fuchida and DeShazer met several times and, as DeShazer said, "We shared in that good wonderful thing that Christ has done."[10]

Jacob DeShazer was liberated from the Japanese prison by American forces a few days after Japan's surrender to America in August 1945. But DeShazer's true liberation occurred earlier—the moment he chose to forgive his captors.

CHAPTER SEVEN

HOW CAN I KNOW HOW TO START OVER WHEN I'VE BLOWN IT?

Pastor, I need to see you right away," John pleaded on the other end of the line. Thirty-five years in the ministry has taught me that such an urgent request for an appointment is never to deliver good news. I hastily rearranged my schedule to counsel with this member of my church who was one of the most respected leaders in our congregation. When he finally arrived for the appointment, I was shocked by his appearance. His face was ashen and his hands trembled as he told the circumstances that had precipitated this meeting.

Over the course of the past year John had been counseling with a female subordinate in his company about some difficulties she was experiencing in her marriage. She and John would meet several times a week for lunch to discuss her issues with her husband. Soon, John began opening up to Karen about the loneliness he felt after twenty years in an unsatisfying relationship. Though there was no physical contact between John and Karen other than an occasional hug, their emotional bond strengthened over the course of several months. Their communication included e-mails throughout the day—some serious and others playful. Sometimes they would text one another late at night after their spouses had gone to bed.

What John did not know was that Karen was also counseling with her pastor, not only about her marital difficulties but also about her growing emotional attachment to John. The pastor convinced Karen that she needed to break off her relationship with John immediately before she lost her marriage. Karen agreed with her pastor's advice and sent an e-mail to John expressing her appreciation for his concern but also her desire to end communication with him. "We both know where this is headed if we don't stop now. Although my marriage is not perfect, it is important to me, and I don't want to add to the problems my husband and I are having. I'm asking that you respect my decision and not attempt to contact me again."

John was devastated. He could not stand the thought of suddenly cutting off communication with someone who had filled an emotional vacuum in his life. He sent her a long e-mail, pleading for a meeting with her. She responded curtly, "I don't want to talk with you. Please don't contact me again." He tried calling her, but she allowed all John's calls to go to voicemail. He would awaken in the middle of the night and text her, but there was no reply.

Two days before John came to see me, his supervisor at work called him in and informed John that Karen had complained that she was being harassed by John's continued attempts to contact her. When John denied the charge, the supervisor reached in his desk drawer and pulled at a file folder containing copies of all of John's attempted contacts with Karen. "John, we are a small company and cannot afford the possibility of a sexual harassment lawsuit. We are going to have to terminate you." John tried to defend his actions, but his supervisor cut him off. "This decision is final. You have one hour to pack your belongings. Our security guard will escort you to your car."

On the long drive home John tried to decide how he would tell his wife, Mary, what had happened—and why. After John gave as brief of a synopsis of the events as he could, Mary sat speechless for what seemed like eternity. Then, she surprised John by saying, "I want to see your phone." At first John tried to dissuade her, saying that no useful purpose could come from looking at the messages he had sent Karen. But she insisted, taking John's phone into the bedroom and shutting the door. John knew what she would find: e-mails and text messages that increased in number and emotional intensity over the last half year, peppered with "I love you" and "I miss you." Some of the messages included John's criticisms of his wife for being "unfeeling" and "unable to meet his needs."

When Mary finally emerged from the bedroom, she said calmly and coldly, "John, I want you to move out of this house now." In one afternoon, John had lost his job, his wife of twenty years, and his reputation—all because of a mistake he had made.

After John related his story to me, he asked a simple question: "Pastor, is there any hope for me?" I understood what he was asking. John was not questioning whether or not his mistake would cause him to forfeit going to heaven when he died. He was a Christian—a well-taught Christian—who knew that genuine believers could never lose their salvation. Nor was John inquiring about the possibility of rescuing his job or restoring his marriage. He knew his job had been terminated and his marriage was on life support.

The question John was really asking was much broader and, in the short term, more consequential: "Can I start over, or must I spend the rest of my life paying for this mistake?" John wasn't doubting God's willingness to allow him into heaven when he died, but he was wondering if he was sentenced to a lifetime of hell while he remained alive on earth.

Maybe you are asking the same question as well. An unwanted divorce, an undeserved termination, an unwise business decision, or an unexpected lapse in judgment has left you sitting on the ash heap of a ruined life wondering, "Can I ever recover from this?" If that is true of you—or someone you know—the good news is that your failure does not have to be the final chapter of your life story. You can recover from the inevitable and seemingly unforgivable mistakes in your life by following these four sequential principles.

PRINCIPLE #1: ADMIT OUR MISTAKES

When our daughter Julia was little she was a fan of *Sesame Street* (I can still hear the theme song in my mind as I type these words!). Her favorite character was Big Bird, whose signature line was "Everybody makes mistakes." One day I confronted my five-year-old daughter with a transgression that demanded severe discipline. As I was getting ready to administer justice, Julia turned around and said, "But Dad, everybody makes mistakes." It's hard to discipline and laugh at the same time!

Big Bird was right. All of us are going to make mistakes. Some of our mistakes are insignificant, like exceeding the speed limit and receiving a ticket. Other failures result in more severe consequences like a wrong investment decision that wipes out our retirement account. But the kind of failures we are talking about in this chapter are major mistakes that alter the course of our life—failures that are the most painful kind to endure because they are self-inflicted. Writer F. B. Meyer captures the agony of such mistakes with these words:

> This is the bitterest thought of all—to know that one's suffering need not have been. To know that it has resulted from indiscretion and inconsistency; that it is the harvest of one's own sowing; that the vulture which feeds on the vitals is a nestling of one's own rearing. Ah, me, this is pain![1]

The lament that accompanies self-inflicted failures always begins with these two words: "If only . . ."

If only I had not clicked on that website.
If only I had stopped the relationship before it was discovered.

If only I had sought help for my addiction before it destroyed me.
If only I had said "I'm sorry" before she died.

The starting place for a new beginning from mistakes that we cannot pin on anyone else is admitting to ourselves—and to our God—that we have indeed failed. That is easier said than done for most of us. We have an inherited predisposition to deny or rationalize failure rather than admit it. Why?

Sometimes pride prevents us from admitting we have failed. We believe that we are immune from the mistakes that other mere mortals make. Yet the truth is we all have inherited a tendency toward failure that is explained by a three-letter word in the Bible: *sin*. The apostle Paul wrote, "All have sinned and fall short of the glory of God" (Romans 3:23). The word *sin* means "to miss the mark." The popularity of the book series and movie *The Hunger Games* has resulted in a renewed interest in archery, which provides a picture of what this word means. An archer who fails to hit the bull's-eye has "missed the mark" regardless of how close he gets. In the same way, all of us will fail to hit God's standard of perfection for any area of life 100 percent of the time—or even most of the time.

Our predisposition to failure is an inherited trait that has been passed down to us from Adam. His initial decision to rebel against God's command in the garden infected every human being after him with this sin virus. Paul explains that inherited predisposition to sin this way:

Therefore, just as through one man [Adam] sin entered into the world, and death through sin, and so death spread to all men, because all sinned. (Romans 5:12)

We can leave it to the theologians to debate the process by which Adam's sin was passed down to us, but one truth is absolutely clear both through the Bible and our everyday experience: every one of us is predisposed toward failure in our marriage, our finances, our moral life, and our relationship to God. While that reality does not exempt us from the consequences of our mistakes, it can serve as an antidote to pride, which prevents us from admitting our mistakes.

Fear is another reason some people cannot admit their failures. When God came looking for Adam after his sin, Adam's first instinct was to hide from God in the trees (kind of futile when you remember God had made the trees!). Why was Adam hiding? "I was afraid," Adam told the Lord (Genesis 3:10). Afraid of what? Adam was paralyzed by the thought of having his failure exposed and spending the rest of his life suffering the consequences for his failure.

That same fear of consequences causes many of us to refuse to admit our mistakes. We are convinced that acknowledging a failure in our work might cost us our job. Acknowledging an immoral relationship will cost us our marriage. Acknowledging an addiction will cost us the loss of our reputation.

So we do everything we can to cover over our mistakes rather than admit them. The problem with cover-ups is that they rarely work. Every day the newspaper is filled with stories about politicians, entertainers, clergymen, and businessmen whose dishonesty and immorality are suddenly exposed. And even if you successfully hide your failure from others, you will never be able to hide your sin from God:

And there is no creature hidden from His sight, but all things are open and laid bare to the eyes of Him with whom we have to do. (Hebrews 4:13)

However, beyond the ineffectiveness of trying to hide failure, there is an even more potent reason for confessing our mistakes: admitting failure is a prerequisite for moving beyond our failure. Pastor and author Gordon MacDonald, who experienced a moral earthquake in his own life many years ago that threatened his marriage and ministry, has written:

> Failures are transformed—or not—depending on the state of our hearts. Some people drench failure with clever euphemisms, wiggle out of responsibility, circumvent consequences and scatter blame with panicked liberality. God requires a radically different response to failure: Failures must be named; consequences accepted.[2]

Solomon offered this blunt observation: "He who conceals his transgressions will not prosper" (Proverbs 28:13). Given the humiliation that Solomon's father, David, experienced when his infamous tryst with Bathsheba was revealed, Solomon could have written, "He who conceals his transgression will ultimately be exposed." But instead of focusing solely on the futility of hiding our mistakes, Solomon points to the benefits of confessing our failure. Only when we admit our failure can we recover and even profit from our failure.

Admitting Our Mistakes Is Essential for Receiving God's Forgiveness

As long as we are clutching our denials or excuses for our failure, we can never receive God's forgiveness. Saint Augustine famously said, "God only gives to those whose hands are empty." We will focus on how to receive God's forgiveness (and why we need it even if we are already a Christian) in the next section.

Admitting Our Mistakes Is Essential for Renewing Our Vitality

Trying to conceal our failure can be taxing. Hiding bills from our mate, trying to remember what story we told to which person, and inventing new excuses to conceal our activities exacts a heavy emotional and physical toll. And then there is the constant, unrelenting fear of discovery that plagues us day and night. King David wrote about the period in his life in which he attempted to conceal his adulterous relationship with Bathsheba. Instead of being a source of exhilaration, David's sin and resulting cover-up was a source of exhaustion:

> When I kept silent about my sin, my body wasted away through my groaning all day long. For day and night Your hand was heavy upon me; my vitality was drained away as with the fever heat of summer. (Psalm 32:3–4)

For anywhere from six months to a year, David did everything within his power—including having Bathsheba's husband killed—to keep his illicit relationship hidden. When the prophet Nathan confronted David with the famous words "Thou art the man" (2 Samuel 12:7 KJV), David knew that everyone else in the kingdom knew about his failure. Yet David was still king and could easily have ordered Nathan executed and the wagging tongues of his subjects silenced.

But David was tired of carrying the twin anvils of guilt and fear on his buckling shoulders. Confession of his failure was the only way to unload the heavy oppression he had felt for far too long. The relief David felt after admitting his sin was immediate:

> I acknowledged my sin to You, and my iniquity I did not hide; I said, "I will confess my transgressions to the LORD"; and You forgave the guilt of my sin. . . . Be glad in the LORD and rejoice, you righteous ones; and shout for joy all you who are upright in heart. (Psalm 32:5, 11)

Admitting Our Mistakes Is Essential for Learning from Our Mistakes

Failure always has a price tag attached to it. Our mistake may cost us our job, our life savings, our most valued friendship, or even our marriage. It is terrible to have to pay for our mistakes. But what is even more tragic is having to pay for the same mistake again!

The Bible uses the term "reproof" to describe the negative consequences that result from our mistakes: bankruptcy, termination from a job, or divorce. Think of a reproof as tuition you pay for taking a course in school. You can learn from the course and graduate, or you can fail the course and have to take it again (and have to pay the tuition again).

Similarly, after we have paid a hefty price for our failures, we can either learn from those failures or repeat them. Throughout the book of Proverbs, Solomon contrasts the wise person who learns from reproofs with the foolish man who ignores reproofs:

> He is on the path of life who heeds instruction, but he who ignores reproof goes astray. (Proverbs 10:17)

> Whoever loves discipline loves knowledge, but he who hates reproof is stupid. (Proverbs 12:1)

> Poverty and shame will come to him who neglects discipline, but he who regards reproof will be honored. (Proverbs 13:18)

Someone has used the word *mistakes* as an acrostic describing benefits that can result from our failures:

> **M**essages that give us feedback about our life;
> **I**nterruptions that should cause us to reflect and think;
> **S**ignposts that direct us to the right path;
> **T**ests that push us toward greater maturity;
> **A**wakenings that keep us in the game mentally;
> **K**eys that we can use to unlock the next door of opportunity;
> **E**xplorations that let us journey where we've never been before;
> **S**tatements about development and progress.[3]

However, for any of these benefits to accrue to our account we must first be willing to admit that we have indeed failed. Until we are willing to admit our mistake, we cannot profit from our mistake. "He who conceals his transgressions will not prosper" (Proverbs 28:13).

Admitting our failures paves the way for the next step toward a new beginning.

PRINCIPLE #2: EXPERIENCE GOD'S FORGIVENESS

I realize that I am writing to two very different audiences who share one common trait: the tendency to make mistakes. First, let me address readers who are not yet Christians. Perhaps you picked up this book or a friend gave it to you because you are seriously considering becoming a follower of Jesus Christ. If you are not a Christian yet and feel overwhelmed by your failure, your need is for God's "judicial" forgiveness, or as it is sometimes called in the Bible, "justification."

The word *justification* is a legal term describing God's action of declaring a person "not guilty" on the basis of Christ's death for his sins. As we saw in the previous chapter, the moment you trust in Jesus Christ alone for your forgiveness, God wraps the perfect righteousness of His Son around you and no longer holds you accountable for your failures. King David expressed the relief that comes from experiencing God's judicial forgiveness:

How blessed is he whose transgression is *forgiven*, whose sin is *covered*! How blessed is the man to whom the LORD does not *impute* iniquity. (Psalm 32:1–2)

The word translated "blessed" means "happy." Three words in these two verses explain the results of God's judicial forgiveness of our sins that results in happiness for the recipient of that forgiveness.

Forgiven

The Hebrew word rendered "forgiven" means "separated." We all have a difficult time separating people from their failures—especially when those failures affect our lives. Take a moment and think of someone who has hurt you deeply in the past. Every time you hear that person's name mentioned in a conversation, what is the first thing you think about? I'll bet it is not that person's positive character qualities! We all tend to link people with their failures. Even after we have forgiven them, we have difficulty separating them from their offenses against us.

Fortunately, God is not like us. When God forgives us, He separates us from our crime against Himself. One of the greatest illustrations of that separation is seen in the Jewish Day of Atonement. Before the high priest would enter the Holy of Holies, he would confess the sins of the people over the head of a goat, known as the scapegoat. Then the goat was dispatched into the wilderness never to be seen again.

When you trust in Christ for the forgiveness of your sins, God places your sins on Jesus Christ—our divine scapegoat, who removes our sin from God's view forever. The psalmist declared, "As far as the east is from the west, so far has He removed our transgressions from us" (Psalm 103:12).

Covered

God's judicial forgiveness also covers our sin. Both Adam and King David illustrate the futility of trying to conceal our mistakes. No matter how hard we try to hide our failure through cover-ups, denials, or rationalizations, our failures keep reappearing like a stubborn stain that will not go away. David, exhausted from his futile attempts to hide his sin from others and from God, cried out in desperation, "Purify me . . . and I shall be clean; wash me, and I shall be whiter than snow" (Psalm 51:7). When we accept Christ's death on the cross as the only adequate payment for our sin against God, the blood of Jesus

Christ acts as a spiritual detergent that eternally erases the stain of our failure.

Imputed

The third result of God's judicial forgiveness is that He will never "impute iniquity" to us. The word translated "impute" is an accounting term that means "to charge to the account of." Every time I write a check (no, I haven't yet succumbed to debit cards), the bank "imputes" that charge to my account. Everything is fine as long as I have enough money in my account to cover the charges. But if the charges exceed my balance, I am overdrawn and in trouble with the bank.

Every sin we commit is like a charge against our spiritual bank account with God. The problem is we never receive any credit for the good things we do since our righteousness is "like a filthy garment" to God (Isaiah 64:6). Our good works are as worthless to God as counterfeit cash is to a bank. So here is the double dilemma we face: We get charged for our sin, but never receive any credit for our good deeds. The result is every hour of every day we continue going deeper and deeper into a deficit position with God.

However, when we trust in Christ for the forgiveness of our sins God deposits into our spiritual bank account all of the perfection of His Son, Jesus Christ. Immediately our sins are paid for, meaning we no longer have to dread the eternal consequences of spiritual bankruptcy. Christ's perfect righteousness is deposited (or "imputed") to our account, and our sins are charged to Jesus Christ. What a deal! As Paul explained "[God] made Him [Jesus] who knew no sin to be sin on our behalf, that we might become the righteousness of God in Him" (2 Corinthians 5:21).

We never have to fear that at some point in the future God is going to ask us to pay for the sins Christ's death has already covered. God will never "impute" our sins to us. God's forgiveness means . . .

- He will never think of your failure when He thinks of you.
- Your mistake has been permanently erased from God's record of your life.
- Your sin will never be called up by God for further review.

No wonder David was so ecstatic over God's forgiveness of his sins!

Christians Need Forgiveness Too

However, I also realize there are some reading this book who are already Christians. You may wonder, *If God has already completely and eternally forgiven me of my sins, why do I need to experience God's forgiveness again after I have failed?*

While God's "judicial forgiveness" is a once-for-all action by which God declares us completely and eternally forgiven, we still need to regularly experience God's "parental forgiveness" for our failures. Every parent (that's many of us) and every child (that's *all* of us) can understand this concept. When your child disobeys you, you probably don't run to your attorney and immediately disinherit your offspring. Even if you did resort to that extreme action, your child would always be your child.

Nevertheless, as long as your child persists in rebelling against you there will be a relational barrier between you and him. The natural guilt he feels over his disobedience makes him reluctant to want to spend time with you. Likewise, as long as he disregards your wishes, you will be less inclined to answer his requests or surprise him with nice gifts.

In the same way, when Christians rebel against God, we do not lose our position in God's family. Once you are "born again" (the term Jesus used in John 3 to describe the result of God's judicial forgiveness) into God's family you cannot become "unborn." However, our failure to obey God raises a relational barrier that creates distance between our heavenly Father and us. As Isaiah said to the

Israelites: "Your iniquities have made a separation between you and your God" (Isaiah 59:2). Isaiah was not addressing heathen nations but Israelites who were already part of God's covenant promises. Although they were part of God's family, their sins had separated them from God's blessings. Similarly, our disobedience toward God does not rob us of our position in God's family, but it does separate us from intimacy with our heavenly Father and many of the benefits that come from Him.

How do we break down that barrier created by our disobedience and restore our relationship with God? In a word: confession. The apostle John described the importance of parental forgiveness for a Christian when he wrote:

> If we say that we have no sin, we are deceiving ourselves and the truth is not in us. If we confess our sins, He is faithful and righteous to forgive us our sins and to cleanse us from all unrighteousness. If we say we have not sinned, we make Him a liar, and His word is not in us. (1 John 1:8–10)

We usually apply the above words to how non-Christians can receive God's judicial forgiveness. But John's letter was written not to unbelievers, but to Christians whom the apostle repeatedly referred to as "little children"—members of God's own family. A Christian who refuses to admit his sin before God is like a young child who insists he never went near the cookie jar while the crumbs are dangling from his mouth as he speaks!

Instead of denying our mistakes, it makes much more sense to confess what both God and we already know: we have failed. When you acknowledge your mistake to God you are not providing Him with any new information! Instead, you are dismantling the relational barrier that has isolated you from God. When that wall is removed, God's forgiveness washes over you, allowing you to experience all the benefits of a restored relationship with Him. Alan Redpath explains the great benefit of simply acknowledging our failure to God:

> It is a tremendous moment in a Christian's life when he can honestly look up into the face of God and say, "Yes, Lord, you are right and I am wrong. Yes, Lord, I got what I deserved in this situation. You are right; I am wrong." That is the thing for which God has been working in your life and in mine from the moment of our conversion.[4]

Why Do Forgiven People Still Hurt?

Although God's forgiveness washes away the eternal and relational consequences of our sin, it does not remove the temporary results of our mistake. Christians who have been forgiven by God still go to prison, experience divorces, suffer from STDs, and deal with estrangement from friends and family members. I am often asked by people who have failed miserably and sought God's forgiveness, "If God has truly forgiven me, why doesn't He erase these painful consequences from my life?"

Experiencing consequences for mistakes is one way that God maintains order in society. A world in which no one ever suffered incarceration for crimes, divorce for adultery, or foreclosure for financial delinquency would be a world filled with chaos. God's universal law of "Whatever a man sows, this he will also reap" (Galatians 6:7) is His primary method for keeping rebellion in check in the world He has created.

Knowing that harsh consequences await us if we disobey God's or man's law discourages our disobedience. Watching others experience harsh results for their disobedience can also serve as a strong deterrent to sin. This is why the apostle Paul commanded that unrepentant leaders in the church be publicly reprimanded: "Those who continue in sin, rebuke in the presence of all, so that the rest also will be fearful of sinning" (1 Timothy 5:20).

God's refusal to remove all of the hurtful effects from our failures—even after we have sought and received His forgiveness—is actually a sign of God's love for us. Even after King David received God's forgiveness for his sin with Bathsheba, he still suffered the aftershocks of a dead child, a disloyal son, and a divided kingdom. Yet David expressed gratitude for those difficult and continuing consequences because they motivated him to obey God: "Before I was afflicted I went astray, but now I keep Your word" (Psalm 119:67).

A woman visiting Switzerland came upon a sheepfold one day. She noticed dozens of sheep seated on the ground, surrounding the shepherd. But in the corner lay a single sheep in a pile of straw, obviously suffering great pain. Upon further inspection she noticed that the sheep's leg was broken. She asked the shepherd what had happened. "I broke it myself," he responded.

Sensing her surprise, the shepherd explained, "Of all the sheep in my flock, this one was the most wayward. It would not obey my voice and often wandered away from the flock. On several occasions it wandered to the edge of a perilous cliff. Not only that, but it was starting to lead other sheep astray as well. I knew I had no choice, so I broke its leg.

"At first the sheep was resentful. When I would attempt to feed it, it nearly bit my hand off. But after a few days it became submissive and obedient. Today, no sheep hears my voice so quickly, nor follows more closely."[5]

Sometimes God may choose to remove the pain of your failure when you receive His forgiveness. But more often His plan is for you to continue to feel the sting of your mistakes—not because God hates you but out of His desire to keep you close to Himself.

PRINCIPLE #3: WAIT FOR GOD'S DIRECTION

New beginnings in life often require us to endure a time of waiting for God's direction. In my book *Second Chance, Second Act* I discuss the concept of "intermissions" in life.[6] An intermission is that time between your failure and your future. It is that lull between:

- your termination from one job and employment in another job;
- your divorce and the beginning of another relationship;
- your bankruptcy and financial solvency.

When we fail, we wonder if the curtain has come down on our life story, never to rise again. But contrary to F. Scott Fitzgerald's observation that "there are no second acts in American lives," God delights in creating second acts for His children. However, experiencing an enjoyable and rewarding second act in our life after a major failure usually requires enduring an intermission.

Most people hate the idea of waiting. Our natural tendency is to want to rush from our last job to our next job or from our last relationship to the next relationship. Yet through the Bible God has always used intermissions in the lives of His people to prepare them for a better future.

The southern kingdom of Judah experienced a seventy-year intermission in exile in Babylon. God used these years between Judah's rebellion against God and her return to Jerusalem as a time to strengthen her relationship with God.

The apostle Peter's intermission was the seven weeks between his denial of Christ in Caiaphas's courtyard until his courageous sermon on the steps of the temple on the Day of Pentecost. During this interval the resurrected Christ appeared to Peter, assured him of His forgiveness, and reminded him of his calling in life (John 21:17).

The apostle Paul experienced a three-year intermission between his transformation from the greatest persecutor of Christianity to the greatest evangelist in the history of the world. During these three years in the desert God personally tutored Paul in the great doctrinal truths he would spend the rest of his life proclaiming.

Moses' intermission lasted forty years. This future liberator of Israel spent the first forty years of his life in Pharaoh's court as a result of God's miraculous protection of his life. He had it all—a great education, powerful rhetorical skills, and a direct line to the most powerful leader in the world.

But God did not utilize Moses' gifts or connections to fulfill His plan to make Moses the catalyst for Israel's exodus from Egypt. Instead, God used Moses' failure. When Moses was about forty years of age, he killed an Egyptian soldier in a moment of unbridled anger. Instantly, life as Moses knew it was over. He would spend the next forty years of his life running from Pharaoh. But Moses' forty years in the desert was simply an intermission during which God taught His servant some invaluable lessons that would prepare him for his second act (which began at age eighty!).

None of us enjoys intermissions. We are ready to rush from our failure into the "next big thing" God has planned for us. However, failing to allow for an interlude between our failure and our second act can have disastrous consequences because of what my friend Bobb Biehl calls "the blizzard effect." A blizzard is the result of tiny particles of snow being driven by a furious windstorm, resulting in blurred visions. By themselves, these bits of frozen precipitation are inconsequential. However, in a storm they can so impair your vision that your safety is jeopardized if you try to travel while the blizzard is blowing.

Divorces, terminations, moral or financial failures, or the loss of a loved one all represent storms in our lives that cause major destruction. When we are in the middle or the immediate aftermath of such a storm, we should not try to make important decisions because our ability to see life clearly has been severely impaired. Instead, we need to allow the winds to die down before we attempt to move forward. Failed second marriages, relapses into addictions, and disastrous financial mistakes are often the result of trying to travel while still in the aftermath of an emotional blizzard.

Although most of us have a built-in aversion to intermissions, it is important to remember that waiting time does not have to be wasted time. Instead of bemoaning intermissions, we can benefit from them if we use these life interludes in helpful ways.

Replenish Our Emotional and Physical Energy

Remember the story of the prophet Elijah? God encouraged him to take a few days off after his exhilarating victory over the false prophets on Mount Carmel and his exhausting run from a vengeful Queen Jezebel. During those days the prophet did nothing other than sleep, eat and drink, and sleep some more. As a result of that time of physical and emotional refreshment, Elijah's perspective was dramatically changed. Prior to his God-imposed intermission, Elijah had been ready to surrender his prophet's badge and die. But after that period of refreshment he was ready to get back to business.

Failure drains our emotional and physical strength. Understanding that reality, God often provides us with an intermission (often against our will) during which we can recharge our depleted emotional and physical batteries, regain our perspective, and eventually resume our life story. Instead of resenting that lull between our failure and our future, see it as a gift from God to prepare you for your second act.

Reflect on Our Failure and Our Future

Intermissions can also provide us with the time to reflect on (not wallow in) our failure so that we don't repeat our mistake. Here are some questions to ask yourself about your failure during your intermission:

- Have I really failed or just fallen short of an unrealistic goal?
- Is my failure the result of other people, adverse circumstances, or my own wrong choices?

- Do I know anyone who has made the same mistake and recovered from it?
- What can I do differently in the future to prevent a similar failure?
- Is there anything in my life that is displeasing to God?

Your intermission can also be a time to reflect on what you believe God wants you to do in the future. Recently a friend of mine was laid off unexpectedly from a job. When he called me with the news on a Thursday afternoon, I suggested that he take a long weekend off with his wife in order to regain his equilibrium after the shock he had experienced. On Monday morning I encouraged him to get up at his normal time, dress, and sit down at his desk at home and answer some key questions that would provide direction for his future:

- What three things would I like to accomplish before I die?
- Am I in the vocation I want to be in ten years from now?
- What do I feel most passionately about in life?
- What do other people think I'm gifted to do?
- What would be an ideal day for me? (Where would I be living, what job would I have, what people would be around me?)

You may be wondering, *Shouldn't I be consulting God, rather than myself, about my future direction*? Of course we should ask God to provide direction for our future! However, the real question is, how will God reveal His answers to you?

One of the most overlooked principles for discovering God's will is that God often directs us through the desires He places in our hearts. The apostle Paul wrote, "For it is God who is at work within you, giving you the will and the power to achieve his purpose" (Philippians 2:13 PHILLIPS). If our primary goal in life is to please God, the Bible promises that God will make His desires our desires. "Delight yourself in the LORD; and He will give you the desires of your heart" (Psalm 37:4). The above questions are a way to discern the true desires of your heart—which many times can also be God's desires for your life.

One final thought: you don't need to wait until you experience a forced intermission to consider the above directional questions. Why not take a day of vacation or a Saturday, turn off the blizzard of activity in your life, and ask God to use these questions to provide His direction for your future?

Once your intermission has concluded, it is time to start over with a new beginning.

Start Over with a New Beginning

While you are in your intermission, it is essential that you develop what I call a "second-act script" so that when God signals your intermission is over, you have a definite plan for a new beginning. Although many Christians think that planning is unspiritual, the writer of Proverbs extolled the benefits of planning:

> Commit your works to the LORD and your *plans* will be established. (Proverbs 16:3)

> Prepare *plans* by consultation, and make war by wise guidance. (Proverbs 20:18)

> The *plans* of the diligent lead surely to advantage, but everyone who is hasty comes surely to poverty. (Proverbs 21:5)

Obviously, any of our plans can be overridden by an all-powerful God. Nevertheless, the reality of God's sovereignty does not negate the importance of developing plans.

Make a Plan

Take a few hours during your intermission, sit down with a legal pad and a cup of coffee, and prepare your second-act script, using this four-part outline.

Clarify the problem. Using a phrase or single word, describe the failure from which you are attempting to recover. It might be "divorce," "addiction," "termination," or "financial failure."

Visualize the goal. In a sentence describe what you would like to happen to resolve this problem. For example, "I would like to have a job that is both rewarding and secure" or "I would like to have enough money so that finances are not a source of constant stress."

Identify barriers. What obstacles are keeping you from your stated goal? Before you can eliminate barriers, you have to identify them. For example, if you are unemployed and desire a satisfying and secure job, you might identify the following barriers to such a job:

- Limited contacts in the vocational field in which you are interested;
- Lack of educational requirements for the job you desire;
- Living in the wrong geographical area of country to pursue this career.

Specify action steps. Once you have identified these major barriers, then you can develop specific action steps to remove them. For example, if a limited number of contacts is a problem, your to-do list might include: having lunch with one or two people you know in your preferred vocational field who could provide additional names, attending a seminar about that vocation to help expand your network, reading articles related to your desired job, and e-mailing either the article's writer or people mentioned within the article for advice. Your action steps will become your to-do list when you are ready to move beyond your intermission into the next phase of your life.

But how can you know when your intermission is truly over?

Be Attentive to Changes

Do you remember the beginning of the movie *Mary Poppins*, in which a weather vane swings 180 degrees signaling to Bert the chimney sweep that a major change is in the air? At the end of the movie, when it is time for Mary Poppins to leave, the weather vane swings again in the opposite direction.

Wouldn't it be helpful if you had your own personal weather vane to alert you when a new chapter of your life was about to begin? Actually, God often uses changes in our life to indicate when our intermission is over and we are ready to begin our second act. Specifically, you should be attentive to changes in . . .

Your attitude. Have you quit blaming others for your failure? Only when you accept your responsibility for your mistakes can you learn from those failures and have a successful second act.

Your emotions. Are you still emotionally and physically exhausted from the fallout from your failure, or are you starting to feel refreshed?

Your circumstances. Often God uses a change in our circumstances to signal that we are ready to begin a new chapter in our life story. That change in circumstances might include an invitation to dinner with someone we are interested in, an unexpected call from a job recruiter about a position that appeals to us, or the departure of your last child from home.

PRINCIPLE #4: GO FORWARD

For Moses and the Israelites the sign that they were about to experience a new chapter in their lives was a dramatic change in Pharaoh's attitude. After refusing Moses's numerous appeals to "Let my people go," Pharaoh relented and wanted to rid Egypt as quickly as possible of those pesky Israelites and the painful plagues their God had sent. Moses and the Israelites took advantage of Pharaoh's sudden policy shift and headed out in the middle of the night on their march toward the Promised Land.

Obviously, Moses and the Israelites knew where they wanted to go. When Pharaoh granted permission for the Israelites to leave, they didn't have to ask for a few days to determine "Where would we like to be living ten years from now?" Their four-hundred-year intermission in Egypt had given them plenty of time to work out their "second-act script" whenever their circumstances changed. When Pharaoh said, "Go!" they were ready to move.

However, a giant obstacle stood between their painful past in Egypt and their promised future in Canaan: the Red Sea. With an Egyptian army pursuing them from behind (Pharaoh had experienced another change of heart and decided he wanted them to remain in Egypt) and a massive body of water in front of them, the Israelites could either be slaughtered or drowned. Not much of a choice. But then God commanded them to do something that seemed absurd:

Tell the sons of Israel to go forward. (Exodus 14:15)

Was God directionally challenged? Going forward meant drowning in the sea God had created. Of course, if you've read the Bible (or seen the movie *The Ten Commandments*) you know what happened next: God miraculously parted the Red Sea, creating a path of dry land on which the Israelites could travel safely to the other side.

I have often reflected on the person in this story who demonstrated the greatest amount of faith. No, it wasn't Moses who was safely on the side with his arms outstretched, striking that Charlton Heston–like pose! To me, the most courageous character in the story was that first Israelite in line who had to step out onto the strip of land that moments earlier had been the bottom of the Red Sea. Think of the faith it took to lead that group between those massive walls of water that could have come crashing down at any moment.

But God had said, "Go forward" and that unnamed Israelite believed that the same God who had miraculously released Israel from Pharaoh's stranglehold could be trusted to deliver them safely to the other side. When God said, "Go," this unsung hero knew it was time for his and Israel's new beginning.

What about you? Are you ready to admit that your failure was primarily your fault and no one else's? Have you acknowledged your mistake to God and received His unconditional forgiveness? Have you taken time to reflect on the cause of your failure as well as the future you would like to experience? If so, don't be surprised if you begin experiencing some major changes in your life that are God's way of telling you, "Go forward." The same God who has brought you to this point will lead you safely to the other side.

That's something you can know for sure!

CHAPTER ONE: HOW CAN I KNOW THERE IS A GOD?

1. Do you think the majority of people in the world actually believe in God or do they "believe in the belief about God"? What about you? What is the difference between believing in God and believing in your belief about God?

2. What do you believe is the best explanation for the growing number of young adults who admit to doubting the existence of God?

3. The author mentions five major sources of doubt about God. Which of those do you believe is the most common reason people question God's existence? Why?

4. Which of the four arguments for the existence of God are most convincing to you: the cosmological, teleological, anthropological, or the experiential? Why? Which of those arguments do you think would be most persuasive for someone you know who doubts God's existence?

5. While acknowledging that all evolutionists are not atheists, the author still claims that the atheistic and evolutionary explanations for the origin of life are the same. Do you think that is fair? Why or why not?

6. The author discusses the risk of not believing in God if He is a reality, but are there similar risks in embracing belief in God if He doesn't exist? Explain your answer.

7. How would you respond to a friend or family member who said to you, "No matter how hard I try, I just cannot accept the idea that there is a God"?

CHAPTER TWO: HOW CAN I KNOW THE BIBLE IS TRUE?

1. How would you respond to someone who said, "It doesn't matter whether the Bible has scientific or historical errors because it is the message of the Bible that is important"?

2. Have you ever doubted the truthfulness of parts of the Bible? If so, which parts have troubled you? How has this chapter helped you resolve those questions?

3. Of the various evidences for the trustworthiness of Scripture explained in this chapter, which one do you find most compelling? Why? Which one do you think would be most persuasive for a non-Christian? Why?

4. How would you answer someone who said, "I don't believe that the writings of Paul are as inspired as the words of Jesus Christ"?

5. The author says that "inspiration" and "inerrancy" only apply to the original manuscripts. Why do you think God didn't preserve those original manuscripts?

6. What do you believe is the greatest difference between the Bible and other religious books such as the Book of Mormon or the Qur'an?

7. If we really believe that the Bible is God's accurate and complete message to us, why don't we read it more frequently?

CHAPTER THREE: HOW CAN I KNOW
CHRISTIANITY IS THE RIGHT RELIGION?

1. Have you ever tried to share your faith with someone who embraces a different religious faith? What was that person's greatest objection to what you were saying?

2. Do you believe people reject the exclusivism of Christianity today more than fifty years ago? Why or why not?

3. How can Christians balance true tolerance with the exclusive claims of Christianity, especially when talking with a non-Christian?

4. Does the fact that the majority of the world embraces other religions ever cause you to doubt that Christianity is the "right" religion? Why or why not? How would you answer someone's question, "How could so many people be wrong?"

5. If God truly loves all people, why would He send to hell people who simply chose the wrong religion?

6. The author mentions several ways Jesus is different from the founders of other major religions. Which of these truths about Jesus is the most powerful argument for Christianity? Why?

7. How would you answer the question, "How can God justly condemn people to hell who have never heard the message of Jesus Christ?" What passages in the Bible would support your answer?

CHAPTER FOUR: HOW CAN I KNOW GOD IS GOOD WITH ALL THE SUFFERING IN THE WORLD?

1. The author begins this chapter with two stories about people who had two very different responses to the problem of evil in the world: one was driven away from God and the other was drawn closer to God. How do you explain those different responses to the same problem?

2. Has a painful experience in your life caused you to question the goodness or the existence of God? Have you resolved that conflict yet? If so, how?

3. Which of the three explanations the author cites do the majority of non-Christians use to reconcile the reality of suffering with the existence of God? Do you think the majority of Christians use the same explanation or a different one? Why?

4. Of the four truths the author says you can cling to when you are in "the tunnel of chaos," which do you find most encouraging? Why?

5. Do you think it is fair to attribute most of the suffering in the world directly or indirectly to sin? Why or why not?

6. Why do you believe so many Christians struggle with the belief that God is in control of all of His creation? Does a belief in God's sovereignty diminish man's responsibility for his choices? Why or why not?

7. If a Christian woman who had been brutally raped asked you, "Why would God allow this to happen to me?" how would you answer? Would your response be any different if she were not a Christian? Why or why not?

CHAPTER FIVE: HOW CAN I KNOW
I'M GOING TO HEAVEN WHEN I DIE?

1. Have you ever doubted that there is life after death? If so, what precipitated that doubt? Have you resolved that doubt? How?

2. Do you believe most people think about their own death very much? Why or why not?

3. Do you find it difficult to embrace the author's belief that the majority of humanity will be in hell, rather than heaven? Why or why not?

4. How would you answer someone's question, "How could a loving God eternally torment people in hell?"

5. The author explains five realities about heaven. Which of these truths surprised you the most? Why?

6. If you were to die tonight, what is the greatest regret you would have about your life up to this point? Since the chances are you will not die tonight, what could you begin doing differently to erase that regret?

7. The author explains and illustrates what it means to "believe in Jesus" for the forgiveness of our sins. Do you believe most Christians have a correct understanding of what that means? Are you confident you have done that?

CHAPTER SIX: HOW CAN I KNOW HOW
TO FORGIVE SOMEONE WHO HAS HURT ME?

1. What are the hardest kinds of offenses to forgive? Why?

2. Do you agree with the author's explanation of Matthew 6:14–15: "For if you forgive others for their transgressions, your heavenly

Father will also forgive you. But if you do not forgive others, then your Father will not forgive your transgressions"? If not, how would you explain Jesus' words, without explaining away His statement?

3. The author identifies four common misunderstandings about forgiveness that prevent people from forgiving. Which of those misunderstandings do you think is the greatest barrier to forgiveness? Why?

4. Do you agree with the author that genuine forgiveness does not always require or result in reconciliation with our offender? Why or why not? Can you support your position from Scripture?

5. What do you believe is the strongest argument for unconditional forgiveness?

6. Is it wise to tell someone who has hurt you that you have forgiven him or her? Why or why not?

7. What is the most important insight you received from this chapter? Why?

CHAPTER SEVEN: HOW CAN I KNOW HOW TO START OVER WHEN I'VE BLOWN IT?

1. Do you have difficulty admitting failure? If so, is pride or fear the major obstacle to confessing your mistakes? Which factor do you think hinders most people from admitting their failures?

2. Why are some of the "reproofs" or negative consequences we experience from sin immediate, while others are delayed?

3. Reflect on your biggest failure in life (up to this point!). What was the most important lesson you learned from your mistake? Do you feel free to share that lesson with others to help them avoid a similar mistake? Why or why not?

4. Before reading this chapter, how would you have answered the question, "Why do forgiven people still have to suffer for their mistakes?" Has this chapter changed your answer to that question? If so, how?

5. What is the longest "intermission" you have ever experienced? Did you use that time profitably? If you experience another intermission in the future, what will you do differently?

6. The author suggests not waiting until a forced intermission to answer some directional questions. Take a moment right now to answer the first question: "What three things would I like to accomplish before I die?"

7. Are you experiencing an intermission in your life right now? Are you sensing any changes in your attitude, emotions, or circumstances that may be signaling it is time for your new beginning to begin? If so, what are those changes?

CHAPTER 1: HOW CAN I KNOW THERE IS A GOD?

1. Frank Newport, Gallup Poll, "More Than 9 in 10 Americans Continue to Believe in God," Last modified June 3, 2011. http://www.gallup.com/poll/147887/Americans-Continue-Believe-God.aspx. Accessed July 26, 2012.

2. Audrey Barrick. "Global Poll: Most Believe in God, Nonbelief Rises," *Christian Post*. Last modified June 3, 2011. http://www.christianpost.com/news/most-americans-still-believe. Accessed July 26, 2012.

3. R. Albert Mohler, Jr. *Atheism Remix: A Christian Confronts the New Atheists* (Wheaton, IL: Crossway, 2008), 47.

4. Mark Buchanan, *Your God Is Too Safe: Rediscovering the Wonder of a God You Can't Control* (Sisters, OR: Multnomah, 2001), 67.

5. John G. Stackhouse Jr., "There Is an Answer to Evil," *Christianity Today*, May 18, 1984, 40.

6. Kurt DeHaan, "Why Would a Good God Allow Suffering" (Grand Rapids: RBC Ministries, 1990).

7. Harold S. Kushner, *When Bad Things Happen to Good People* (New York: HarperCollins, 1981), 43–44.

8. Richard Dawkins, *The God Delusion* (Boston: Houghton Mifflin, 2006), 100.

9. Tim Keller, *The Reason for God: Belief in an Age of Skepticism* (New York: Riverhead Books, 2008), 87.

10. Alvin Plantinga, *Warranted Christian Belief* (New York: Oxford University Press, 2000), 406. Plantinga cites an important article by the philosopher William Alston, who argues that one can perfectly well do science even if one thinks God has done and even sometimes still does miracles. See "Divine Action: Shadow or Substance?" in *The God Who Acts: Philosophical and Theological Explorations*, Thomas F. Tracy, ed. (Pennsylvania State University Press, 1994), 49–50.

11. Sue Bohlin, Probe Ministries, "There Is No Evidence for God or the Bible." Last modified 2011. http://www.probe.org/site/c.fdKEIMNsEoG/b.4222751/k.F312/There_Is_No_Evidence_for_God_or_the_Bible.htm. Accessed July 26, 2012.

12. Got Questions Ministries, "Is There an Argument for the Existence of God?" Last modified 2012. http://www.gotquestions.org/argument-existence-God.html. Accessed July 26, 2012.

13. Norman L. Geisler and Frank Turek, *I Don't Have Enough Faith to Be an Atheist* (Wheaton, IL: Crossway, 2004), 108–9.

14. James Emory White, *Can We Believe in God?* (Downers Grove, IL: InterVarsity, 2010), 11.

15. Georges Lemaître, The Beginning of the World from the Point of View of Quantum Theory, *Nature* 127 (1931), n. 3210, 706.

16. St. Johns College, University of Cambridge, "Hoyle on the Radio: Creating the 'Big Bang'," http://www.joh.cam.ac.uk/library/special_collections/hoyle/exhibition/radio. Accessed September 12, 2012.

17. Smoot Group Cosmology, press release on 2006 Nobel Prize, http://aether. lbl.gov/press.html. Accessed September 12, 2012. For more on COBE and its successor satellite, the Microwave Anisotropy Probe (MAP), see James Glanz, "In Big Bang's Echoes, Clues to the Cosmos." *New York Times*, February 6, 2001. http://www.nytimes.com/2001/02/06/science/in-big-bang-s-echoes-clues-to-the-cosmos.html?pagewanted=1. Accessed September 12, 2012.

18. William Lane Craig, "Why I Believe God Exists," in *Why I Am a Christian: Leading Thinkers Explain Why They Believe*, Norman Geisler and Paul Hoffman, eds. (Grand Rapids: Baker Books, 2001), 63.

19. Ibid., 64.

20. Mark Mittelberg, *The Questions Christians Hope No One Will Ask: With Answers* (Carol Stream, IL: Tyndale, 2010), 9–10.

21. Ibid.

22. Geisler and Turek, *I Don't Have Enough Faith*, 111.

23. Dennis McCallum, *Christianity: The Faith that Makes Sense* (Canada: Living Books, 1997), 47–48.

24. William Dembski, *Intelligent Design: The Bridge Between Science & Theology* (Downers Grove, IL: InterVarsity, 1999).

25. Ibid.

26. Marilyn Adamson, Every Student.com, "Is There Really a God?: Does God exist? Here Are Six Straight-forward Reasons to Believe That God Is Really There." Last modified 2012. Accessed July 26, 2012. www.everystudent.com/features/isthere.html.

27. Mittelberg, *The Questions Christians Hope No One Will Ask*, 12.

28. Hugh Ross, "Why I Believe in Divine Creation," in Norman Geisler and Paul Hoffman, eds., *Why I Am a Christian*, 138–41.

29. Michael J. Behe, *Darwin's Black Box: The Biochemical Challenge to Evolution* (New York: The Free Press, 1996), in Tom Woodward, "Meeting Darwin's Wager," *Christianity Today,* April 28, 1997, 14.

30. Sir Frederick Hoyle, "Hoyle on Evolution," *Nature* 294, no. 5837 (12 November 1981): 148.

31. Gordon Rattray Taylor, *The Great Evolution Mystery* (New York: Harper & Row, 1983), 101–2.

32. Ibid.

33. Geisler, *I Don't Have Enough Faith*, 108.

34. Charles Colson, *Kingdoms in Conflict* (Grand Rapids: Zondervan, 1987), 28.

35. Allan Sandage, quoted in George Johnson, "Science and Religion: Bridging the Great Divide," *The New York Times* (30 June 1998).

36. J. P. Moreland, "Does the Existence of the Mind Provide Evidence for God?" in *The Apologetics Study Bible* (Nashville: Holman Bibles, 2007), 625.

37. C. S. Lewis, *Mere Christianity* (San Francisco: Harper, 2001), 136.

38. Tim Keller, *The Reason for God*, 159.

39. Chad Brand. "Intellectuals Who Found God," in *The Apologetics Study Bible* (Nashville: Holman Bibles, 2007), 975.

40. A. N. Wilson, Daily Mail (London), "Why We Should No Longer Be Cowed by the Religion of Hatred." www.dailymail.co.uk/news/article-1169145/Religion-hatred-Why-longer-cowed-secular-zealots.html. Last modified April 11, 2009. Accessed July 26, 2012.

41. Got Questions Ministries, "Is There an Argument for the Existence of God?"

42. Ibid.

CHAPTER 2: HOW CAN I KNOW THE BIBLE IS TRUE?

1. The Barna Group, "Americans Identify What They Consider 'Holy' Books." www.barna.org/faith-spirituality/31-americans-identify-what-they-consider-qholyq-books?q=bible stands alone. Last modified July 7, 2008. Accessed July 26, 2012.

2. David Kinnaman, The Barna Group, "New Research Explores How Different Generations View and Use the Bible." www.barna.org/faith-spirituality/317-new-research-explores-how-different-generations-view-and-use-the-bible?q=generational+similarities. Last modified October 19, 2009. Accessed July 26, 2012.

3. Dan Brown, The Da Vinci Code (New York: Doubleday, 2003), 231.

4. Charles Ryrie, What You Should Know about Inerrancy (Chicago: Moody Press, 1981), 30.

5. Charles Ryrie, "A Synopsis of Bible Doctrine," The Ryrie Study Bible NASB (Chicago: Moody Press, 1978), 1933.

6. William Lane Craig, Leadership U, "A Middle Knowledge Perspective on Biblical Inspiration." www.leaderu.com/offices/billcraig/docs/menmoved.html?vm=r. Last modified November 8, 2005. Accessed July 27, 2012.

7. Saint Augustine, Christian Classics Ethereal Library, "The Confessions and Letters of St. Augustine." www.ccel.org/ccel/schaff/npnf101.vii.1.LXXXII.html. Last modified July 13, 2005. Accessed July 27, 2012.

8. William Barclay, Daily Study Bible, Letters to the Galatians and Ephesians, (London: Westminster, 1976), chap. "Women in Greece."

9. John Calvin, Puritan Rising, "John Calvin on the Duty of Kingdoms to Submit to Christ." http://puritanrising.com/2012/02/john-calvin-on-the-duty-of-kingdoms-to-submit-to-christ/. Last modified February 18, 2012. Accessed July 27, 2012.

10. John Wesley, The Journal of John Wesley, 8 Volumes, (London: Epworth Press, 1938), 6:1, 17.

11. Kirsopp Lake, The Religion of Yesterday and Tomorrow (Boston: Houghton, 1926), 61–62. Quoted in Kenneth S. Kantzer, "Why I Still Believe the Bible Is True," Christianity Today, October 7, 1988, 25.

12. Peter W. Stoner, Science Speaks (Chicago: Moody Press, 1958), 100–7.

13. Ken Woodward, "In the Beginning, There were the Holy Books," Newsweek, February 11, 2002. www.bintjbeil.com/articles/en/020211_islam.html. Accessed July 27, 2012.

14. A. W. Pink, The Divine Inspiration of the Bible (Swengel, PA: Bible Truth Depot, 1917), 85.

15. Erwin W. Lutzer. *Seven Reasons Why You Can Trust the Bible* (Chicago: Moody Press, 2001), 51.

16. J. P. Moreland, interviewed by Lee Strobel, *The Case for Christ* (Grand Rapids: Zondervan, 1998), 250.

17. John Gartstang, as quoted in Josh McDowell. *The New Evidence that Demands a Verdict* (Orlando, FL: Here's Life Publishers, 1999), 95.

18. Ibid., 97–98.

19. Ibid., 63.

20. Clifford Wilson, "The Most Unique Book on Earth," *The Apologetics Study Bible* (Nashville: Holman Bible Publishers, 2007), 362.

21. Nelson Glueck, *Rivers in the Desert: History of the Negev* (Philadelphia: Jewish Publications Society of America, 1969), 31.

22. A. T. Robertson, as quoted in Ravi Zacharias and Norman Geisler, *Who Made God?: And Answers to Over 100 Other Tough Questions of Faith* (Grand Rapids: Zondervan, 2003), 127.

23. Arthur Patzia, as quoted in Wendy Murray Zoba, "When Manuscripts Collide." *Christianity Today,* October 23, 1995, 30.

24. Brown, *The Da Vinci Code*, 231.

25. Norman Geisler, "How Can We Know the Bible Includes the Correct Books?" *The Apologetics Study Bible* (Nashville: Holman Bible Publishers, 2007), 724.

26. Ron Mehl, *The Ten(der) Commandments* (Sisters, OR: Multnomah, 1998), 32–33.

CHAPTER 3: HOW CAN I KNOW CHRISTIANITY IS THE RIGHT RELIGION?

1. The Barna Group, "What Americans Believe About Universalism and Pluralism." www.barna.org/faith-spirituality/484-what-americans-believe-about-universalism-and-pluralism?q=americans believe universalism. Last modified 18 April 2011. Accessed July 27, 2012.

2. Randy Alcorn, *If God Is Good* (Colorado Springs, CO: Multnomah, 2009), 219.

3. R. Kirby Godsey, *Is God a Christian?: Creating a Community of Conversation* (Macon, GA: Mercer University Press, 2011), as quoted in an interview by Timothy Dalrymple, "God Is Not a Christian," August 15, 2011. http://www.patheos.com/Resources/Additional-Resources/God-is-Not-a-Christian-Timothy-Dalrymple-08-16-2011.html. Accessed July 27, 2012.

4. Ibid.

5. Robert Jeffress, *Twilight's Last Gleaming* (Nashville: Worthy, 2011).

6. Webster's New World Dictionary, Second College Edition, s.v. "tolerance."

7. Dinesh D'Souza, *What's So Great About Christianity* (Washington, D.C.: Regnery Publishing, 2007), 278.

8. Richard Dawkins, *A Devil's Chaplain: Reflections on Hope, Lies, Science, and Love* (New York: Mariner Books, 2004), 150.

9. Ravi Zacharias, *Jesus Among Other Gods: The Absolute Claims of the Christian Message* (Nashville: Word, 2000), 7.
   Bruce Nicholls, "Is Jesus the Only Way to God?" *Evangelical Review of Theology* 22, no. 3 (July 1998): 228.

10. Ibid.
11. Thomas Paine, as quoted in Josh McDowell, *The New Evidence That Demands a Verdict* (Nashville: Thomas Nelson, 1999), 119.
12. Sura, "The Night Journey," in N. J. Dawood, trans. *The Qur'an* (Baltimore, MD: Penguin, 1972), 235.
13. Ibid.
14. Robert O. Ballou, *The Portable World Bible: A Comprehensive Selection from the Eight Great Sacred Scriptures of the World* (NY: The Viking Press, 1968), 134, 147, 151.
15. C. S. Lewis, *Mere Christianity* (New York: HarperCollins, 1952), 54–56.
16. Josh McDowell and Don Stewart, "How Can You Say That Jesus Is the Only Way to Get to God?" *Discipleship Journal*, March/April 1997, 49.
17. Lewis, *Mere Christianity*, 35.
18. Philip Yancey, *What's So Amazing About Grace?* (Grand Rapids: Zondervan, 1997), 45.
19. C. S. Lewis, "The Higher Place of Faith." *Charisma*, February 12, 2012. http://www.charismamag.com/610-j15/spiritled-woman/spiritled-woman/14904--the-higher-place-of-faith. Accessed July 27, 2012.

CHAPTER 4: HOW CAN I KNOW GOD IS GOOD
WITH ALL THE SUFFERING IN THE WORLD?

1. Bart Ehrman, *God's Problem: How the Bible Fails to Answer Our Most Important Question—Why We Suffer* (New York: HarperOne, 2008), 2–3.
2. Joni Eareckson Tada, "When Life Isn't Fair," *Discipleship Journal*, September/October 1995, 25–30.
3. The OmniPoll, conducted by Barna Research Group, Ltd., January 1999. Cited in Lee Strobel, *The Case for Faith* (Grand Rapids: Zondervan, 2000), 29.
4. David Hume, as quoted in Ravi Zacharias and Norman L. Geisler, *Who Made God?: And Answers to Over 100 Other Tough Questions of Faith* (Grand Rapids: Zondervan, 2003), 35.
5. Mary Baker Eddy, *Science and Health with Key to the Scriptures* (Boston: Church of Christ Scientist, 1994), 124.
6. Reginald S. Luhman, "Belief in God and the Problem of Suffering," *The Evangelical Quarterly*, October 1985, 331.
7. Gordon MacDonald, "The Soul of Steve Jobs," *Leadership Journal*, January 23, 2012, 21.
8. Ravi Zacharias, *Can Man Live Without God?* (Nashville: Thomas Nelson, 2004), 182.
9. Harold S. Kushner, *When Bad Things Happen to Good People* (New York: HarperCollins, 1981), 43–44.
10. Ibid.
11. Elie Wiesel, quoted in Philip Yancey, *Disappointment with God* (Grand Rapids: Zondervan, 1992), 208.
12. Clark Pinnock, "God Limits His Knowledge," in *Predestination and Free Will*, David Basinger and Randall Basinger, eds. (Downers Grove, IL: InterVarsity, 1986), 150.

13. Steve Farrar, *Overcoming Overload: Seven Ways to Find Rest in Your Chaotic World* (Sisters, OR: Multnomah, 2004), 189.

14. C. H. Spurgeon, *The Treasury of the Bible, The Old Testament*, vol. 4 (Grand Rapids: Zondervan, 1962), 212.

15. Donald Grey Barnhouse, *Romans Vol. 3: God's Grace, God's Freedom, God's Heirs* (Grand Rapids: 1983), 158.

16. Charles Swindoll, *The Mystery of God's Will* (Nashville: Word Publishing, 1999), 91.

17. John Ortberg, *Faith and Doubt* (Grand Rapids: Zondervan, 2008), 117–18.

18. Dinesh D'Souza, *What's So Great About Christianity* (Washington, DC: Regnery Publishing, 2007), 278.

19. Ibid.

20. Bob and Gretchen Passantino, "If God Is Good, Why Is There So Much Suffering?" *Discipleship Journal*, March/April 1997, 52.

21. Norman Geisler, "The Problem of Evil," *Baker Encyclopedia of Christian Apologetics* (Ada, MI: Baker, 1999).

22. Dinseh D'Souza, "Why We Need Earthquakes," *Christianity Today*, May 2009, 58.

23. Alister McGrath, *Mystery of the Cross* (Grand Rapids: Zondervan, 1990).

24. Joni Eareckson Tada and Steve Estes, *When God Weeps: Why Our Sufferings Matter to the Almighty* (Grand Rapids: Zondervan, 2000).

25. John Ortberg, *Know Doubt: The Importance of Embracing Uncertainty in Your Faith* (Grand Rapids: Zondervan, 2009), 164.

26. Philip Yancey, *Reaching for the Invisible God* (Grand Rapids: Zondervan, 2002), 95.

CHAPTER 5: HOW CAN I KNOW I'M GOING TO HEAVEN WHEN I DIE?

1. Philip Yancey, *Rumors of Another World* (Grand Rapids: Zondervan, 2003), 228–29.

2. Ernest Becker, *The Denial of Death* (New York: Free Press, 1997), xvii.

3. William Hasker, Stanford University, "Afterlife." http://plato.stanford.edu/entries/afterlife/. Last modified July 6, 2010. Accessed July 27, 2012.

4. Todd Burpo and Lynn Vincent, *Heaven Is for Real: A Little Boy's Astounding Story of His Trip to Heaven and Back* (Nashville: Thomas Nelson, 2010).

5. Don Piper, *90 Minutes in Heaven: A True Story of Death and Life* (New York: Revell, 2004).

6. Peter Kreeft, Leadership U, "The Case for Life After Death." http://www.leaderu.com/truth/1truth28.html. Last modified July 14, 2002. Accessed July 27, 2012.

7. Philip Yancey, "How Dirty Jokes and Fear of Death Prove There is a Heaven," *Christianity Today*, March 2, 1984, 78.

8. Rob Bell, *Love Wins: A Book About Heaven, Hell, and the Fate of Every Person Who Ever Lived* (New York: HarperOne, 2012), xiii.

9. Ibid., 107.

10. Eric Marrapodi, CNN, "Rob Bell Punches Back Against Claims of Heresy." http://religion.blogs.cnn.com/2011/03/19/rob-bell-punches-back-against-claims-of-heresy/. Last modified March 19, 2011. Accessed July 27, 2012.

11. Randy Alcorn, *In Light of Eternity: Perspectives on Heaven* (Colorado Springs: Waterbrook Press, 1999), 39.

12. Ibid., 40.

13. Ibid., 74.

14. Andrew Sullivan, "Christianity in Crisis." *Newsweek*, April 2, 2012. http://www.thedailybeast.com/newsweek/2012/04/01/andrew-sullivan-christianity-in-crisis.html. Accessed July 27, 2012.

CHAPTER 6: HOW CAN I KNOW HOW
TO FORGIVE SOMEONE WHO HAS HURT ME?

1. C. S. Lewis, *Mere Christianity* (New York: Macmillan, 1952), 104.

2. David W. Augsburger, *Cherishable: Love & Marriage* (Harrisonburg, VA: Herald Press, 1975).

3. Gary Thomas, "The Forgiveness Factor," *Christianity Today*, January 10, 2000, 38.

4. Ibid.

5. Lewis B. Smedes, "Forgiveness, The Power to Change the Past," *Christianity Today*, January 7, 1983, 26.

6. Kathy E. Dahlen, "Free to Forgive," *Discipleship Journal*, May/June 1998, 66.

7. Smedes, "Forgiveness," 26.

8. Allen Guezlo, "Fear of Forgiving," *Christianity Today*, February 8, 1993, 43–44.

9. Richard Goldstein, "Jacob DeShazer, Bombardier on Doolittle Raid, Dies at 95." *New York Times*, March 23, 2008. www.nytimes.com/2008/03/23/us/23deshazer.html?pagewanted=print. Accessed July 27, 2012.

10. Ibid.

CHAPTER 7: HOW CAN I KNOW HOW TO START OVER WHEN I'VE BLOWN IT?

1. F. B. Meyer, *Christ in Isaiah* (Fort Washington, PA: Christian Literature Crusade, 1941).

2. Gordon MacDonald, "Transforming Failure," *Discipleship Journal*, January/February 1999. http://www.navpress.com/magazines/archives/article.aspx?id=11565. Accessed July 27, 2012.

3. John Maxwell, *Failing Forward: Turning Mistakes into Stepping Stones for Success* (Nashville: Thomas Nelson, 2007), 53.

4. Alan Redpath, *Victorious Christian Service* (Santa Ana, CA: Calvary Chapel Publishing, 2005), 160.

5. Donald Campbell, *Daniel: Decoder of Dreams* (Colorado Springs: Victor, 1981), 49.

6. Some of the material in this chapter is adapted from my book *Second Chance, Second Act* (Colorado Springs: Waterbrook Press, 2007), which explains in more detail the process of experiencing a new beginning.

About the Author

Dr. Robert Jeffress (DMin, Southwestern Theological Seminary; ThM, Dallas Theological Seminary) is an author and the senior pastor of the eleven-thousand-member First Baptist Church of Dallas, Texas. His bold, biblical, and practical approach to ministry has made him one of the country's most respected evangelical leaders and earned him a Daniel Award from Vision America. He regularly appears on major mainstream media outlets such as Fox News, CNN, MSNBC, *The O'Reilly Factor*, *Cavuto on Business*, ABC's *Good Morning America*, and CBS's *The Early Show*. Dr. Jeffress also hosts a television program, *Pathway to Victory*, and teaches a sermon series that airs daily on 722 radio stations, 1,200 television stations and cable systems, and in 28 countries around the world.

WORTHY®

P U B L I S H I N G

IF YOU ENJOYED THIS BOOK, WILL YOU CONSIDER SHARING THE MESSAGE WITH OTHERS?

- Mention the book in a Facebook post, Twitter update, Pinterest pin, or blog post.

- Recommend this book to those in your small group, book club, workplace, and classes.

- Head over to facebook.com/fbcdallas, "LIKE" the page, and post a comment as to what you enjoyed the most.

- Tweet "I recommend reading #howcaniknow by @robertjeffress // @worthypub"

- Pick up a copy for someone you know who would be challenged and encouraged by this message.

- Write a review on amazon.com or bn.com.

You can subscribe to Worthy Publishing's newsletter at
www.worthypublishing.com

**WORTHY PUBLISHING
FACEBOOK PAGE**

**WORTHY PUBLISHING
WEBSITE**